CW01502211

# INVINCIBLE
# 8 Secrets to Being Happy

# INVINCIBLE
# 8 Secrets to Being Happy

MANUEL BUENO ABALO

# INDEX

To my children. And to Beatriz.

ACKNOWLEDGEMENTS
To those who, through their efforts, have
brought the most beautiful things out of the
darkness to show them to us.

# INTRODUCTION

H appiness is not a gift bestowed by fortune. Instead, it is achieved through effort.

In the chapters that follow, our sage (let's call him Seneca 2.0) rejuvenates his ancient words and talks to eight current people, advising them on how we should lead our lives in order to be free and happy.

We come into the world without understanding our role in this life, and we risk wasting it if we allow ourselves to be led by the herd. Freeing ourselves from the cultural and social pressures that paralyse us will not be easy, but from the very moment we were conceived we were granted the chance to choose what to do with our lives. So, let us exercise that power to navigate life freely and with a calm sense of joy.

From the moment we accept that changing our existence is necessary, we will begin to live in freedom. And from there, we can come to appreciate the beauty of everything around us, which will allow us to have more respect for ourselves and, above all, others.

Whatever may happen will happen for the best of reasons. So, let us enjoy the journey without fear. Most of the time, fear, anger, illness, and even desire are out of our control, so let us understand that what is most precious and what leads to true happiness is already within us.

As you read these pages, you will learn how to face death, how to use wealth, how to help, how not to be a slave either to passion or fear, how to enjoy your leisure time, how to face adversity, how life is short if we do not make good use of the time we have been given. And, above all, you will learn how to be happy.

Only a virtuous people are capable of freedom
BENJAMIN FRANKLIN

# I. TO THE TENACIOUS

"No man is more unhappy than he who never faces adversity."

I t is with pleasure and approval that I see the tenacity and effort with which you try to become a better person every day. Not only do I urge you to persevere in this; I implore you to do so. However, let me give you this piece of advice: avoid certain attention-grabbing attitudes in your way of life, the kind displayed by those who desire admiration rather than inner progress.

Why do we experience setbacks? Adversity is a natural part of life. It must be accepted and overcome.

Just as rivers flow into the sea without impacting on its temperature or salinity, adversity will come to us – but it should not alter us. A steadfast person will keep their balance and overcome misfortunes, because they are stronger than their circumstances; any adversity will be a test and experience of courage.

I do not mean to say that this adversity is not felt, but rather that the person is able to conquer it. Calm and serene, he will rebuff it, taking its evils as proof of his steadfastness. Who is he who is known as brave and calls himself a man, and yet does not wish to face fate, even in the uncertainty of the outcome? Who is he who is known as dedicated, for whom the armchair is not a punishment? Elite athletes do not remain idle, because idleness is a punishment for them. Instead, they constantly seek to compete with and face the strongest in order to know their limits. They cannot prove how great and powerful they are until they have won. What value would your victories have if you had no opponents, and were awarded a trophy just for showing up? You would feel unhappy, because there would have been no rivals to test you and show you your limits.

We should know that good people behave in this way. They are not frightened by adverse and difficult circumstances, nor do they complain about fate; whatever happens to us, we must take it as good, turn it into good. What matters is not what you endure, but how you endure it.

Good parents instruct their children to start their homework early in the morning. They do not release them from work and commitments at weekends, they push them to what they consider their limits to be, even to the point of tears. Meanwhile, bad parents want to keep them close on their laps. They do not allow them to play out in the street, be sad, cry or toil. Fate wants the best for us and, like good parents, trains us with toil, suffering and loss so that we can acquire our true strength. Those who are allowed to do so grow fat in apathy and decay, not only because of their work, but also because of their own movement and their own weight. Undeserved prosperity cannot endure the slightest blow; he who has continuously struggled against adversity has hardened his soul. Even if it is his turn to fall, he will fight on his knees. Does it seem strange to you that fate, who loves the best, delivers setbacks to train you? It doesn't surprise me to see the best fighting against the odds.

I see that you follow my advice when I hear that you have learned to enjoy suffering. Navigating life calmly and with fortune on our side is to delude ourselves about what life is.

Continuing my argument, I will prove that what appears to be bad is not necessarily bad. For now, I will assert that what you may call adversity, misfortune or hardship are all in reality advantages, both for those who suffer them, and for all mankind. I would add that misfortune happens according to destiny, and it happens to the best by virtue of them being the best. After this, I will persuade you that you should never pity a good person, because they might be called unhappy when they are not.

Of all the proposals I have put forward, the first seems to be the most difficult to prove; namely, that the things which horrify and disturb us are actually beneficial to those who endure them. The expressions I remember best and that still live on in my memory include the one that states that "no man is more unhappy than he who never faces adversity". In effect, he has not had the chance to put himself to the test.

Courage seeks out adversity and focuses more on overcoming it than the harm it may cause, because pain is part of glory. Warriors take pride in their wounds and boast of the blood that flows from them for an honourable reason. Brave soldiers who return unharmed from war receive less glory than those who return wounded.

Is he unhappy, he who abandoned fame to dig the earth with his hands, first to fight in order to triumph in the playing fields and now against greed, and because, sitting by the fire, the old victor eats the food that he himself has plucked from the ground? Would he be happier if he filled his stomach with fish from distant shores, the most exotic fruits or the most delicate meats? Is Socrates unhappy because he sipped from the drink allocated to him by the State, as if it were a potion for immortality, and debated death until his own death? Providence will test your mettle in adversity; you will value a pilot in a storm, a soldier in a battle, or you, a direct descendant of Hercules, paying homage to the valour of the gods in your competitions.

Achieving the things you have striven for will make you happy, but remembering the work required to achieve them will make you even happier. Great soldiers enjoy adversity, as do great people like you.

It is admirable how you honour your family and enjoy their presence. You were able to overcome a divorce, but I beg you, do not be frightened by the things providence applies like a sting to our souls. Adversity is an opportunity for courage.

How will I know how you will face poverty if you wallow in wealth? How can I say with what steadfastness you will face hardship, public hatred and dishonour if you grow old surrounded by applause, if people adore you, and you are the man mothers dream of for their daughters? How will I know with what equanimity you would endure the loss of your children if you don't have them? I have heard you offering consolation others; if you had been offering it to yourself, if you had been telling yourself not to lament, then I could have seen your true character.

It is those who are dulled by an excess of fortune and remain calmly standing in a tranquil sea who will rightfully be called unhappy. When something happens to them, they will be helpless. Adversity will most distress those who have endured it the least. A new recruit will turn pale at the thought of the wound while the veteran, who knows that blood goes hand in hand with victory, will gain only more courage at the sight of it gushing forth. For all of these people, who have been blissful for a long time, their time will come.

Remember the wisdom of your elders when they remind you to flee from luxury, from the prosperity that softens minds, which sink into endless inebriation if nothing intervenes to remind them of their human condition. He whose windows protect him from the wind, whose home is always warm, who lives in permanent prosperity, cannot endure a light breeze without sensing danger.

While all excess is pernicious, good fortune is the worst of all. It excites the brain, evokes vain fantasies and generates an intense fog that makes it impossible to differentiate between falsehood and truth. Would it not be better to endure misfortune with the help of courage than be bursting with infinite goods? Dying of hunger is gentle, but when men reach their limits they explode.

The gods follow the same rule with good people as teachers do with their pupils: they demand more effort from those of whom they have higher expectations. In that case, why should it be strange that providence should employ severity when testing the spirits of those of whom it expects the most? Testing courage is never easy. If fortune strikes and hammers us, we must endure it; it is not cruelty, but a test. The more often we go through it, the stronger we will be. The firmest part of the body is that which is constantly used. We must offer ourselves to fortune so that as it oppresses us, it hardens us. Gradually, it will make us equal to it and the frequency of danger will make us rebuff it.

Sailors' bodies are hardened to withstand the sea, just as farmers' hands are toughened by their labour. Soldiers' muscles are vigorous so they can throw spears, and your mind is tenacious so you can prevail in your contests. In each of us, our strongest limb is the one we have exercised.

23

Enduring suffering is the best way for our mind to come to rebuff it.

Is it any wonder, then, that good men are shaken so that they may grow strong? No tree is strong and firm unless it is shaken by strong winds, because it is hardened by the very act that causes it violence and forces it to dig its roots in more firmly. Trees that grow in a sunny valley are fragile. Therefore, it is beneficial to good men to live long in the midst of adversity, so that they may not be afraid, and may learn to bear with composure what is only considered misfortune by those who cannot tolerate it well.

I remember hearing these words:

"I have only one complaint," he said, "against you, immortal gods: it is that you did not tell me your will beforehand, for in that case I would have anticipated these situations for which I now stand trial, called by you. Do you want to take my children? I raised them for you. Do you want any part of my body? Take it; it is no great thing that I offer to you: soon I must leave it all behind. Do you want my life? How can I delay giving you what you have given me? I will gladly put whatever you ask of me in your hands. I would rather have offered you these things than have to return them to you. Why did you need to take them from me? I could have given you them. But even now you cannot take anything from me, for a man cannot be robbed unless he resists."

Destiny guides us. Within the first hour of birth, it was determined how long each of us has to live; one thing hangs on another, and all matters, public and private, are bound by the chains of destiny. We must therefore bear everything with composure. Things do not appear suddenly along the way as we might suppose; rather, they come as arranged. A long time ago, it was determined what would make you laugh, what would make you cry. Although people's lives seem to differ from one another in great variety, the end total is the same: what we receive is fleeting, and soon we will perish. So why complain? Why lament? We are prepared for our destiny; we were born for this. Let nature take care of our bodies as she pleases; let us be cheerful and courageous, whatever happens, and let us think that nothing of our own is in danger. What makes a good man? Offering oneself to destiny, for it is a profound consolation to be uprooted alongside the universe.

Now let us look at an example of bravery. See how in ancient times they believed that the sun stung its son to offer its rays to men, how far courage must rise, and you will see that it cannot be reached by safe roads:

> The start of the journey is arduous, even for well-rested horses in the early morning. In the middle the soaring sky is found, from where, as I gaze at the land and the sea, my body trembles and my heart explodes in my chest. The end is sloping and some braking is needed. When I bathe in its waves, the ancient Thetis fears I will fall.
>
> Having heard this, the brave boy does not shrink away. "I do not fear the road: I get in the chariot. It is worth going to these places, even if you might fall."
>
> And the father never stops trying to intimidate his spirit. "And so as not to deviate from the road, you will pass through the horns of the violent Bull of Taurus, the fierce Lion of Leo and the bow of Sagittarius."

After this, the boy said, "Hitch the cart. I am inspired by those things that you think frighten me, because I enjoy being where even the sun itself trembles."

Seeking safety is for cowards and the weak; courage seeks challenges and new heights.

Some say that many sad, difficult things

happen to them. As it is destiny that placed them in the road, it also armed our spirits against them. Let us bear them with composure.

Disregard poverty, for nobody is as poor as when they were born.

Disregard pain, for it either ends, or ends you.

Disregard fortune, because I gave her no weapon with which she could reach your spirit.

Disregard death, which either finishes you or changes your place.

# II. TO THE BRAVE

"He who does not control his laughter shows more greatness of spirit than he who does not control his tears."

Christine

When I examine myself, I realise that I have faults, some of which are very clear, others a little more diffuse. These I think are the most bothersome, and they attack me like an enemy when they see an opportunity. I do not know whether to be alert, as in war, or unconcerned, as in peace.

Nevertheless, the main defect I find in myself (and why should I not confess the truth to you, as I do to my doctor?) is that I have not entirely freed myself from the things I feared and hated, nor have I submitted to them. I am in a strange state; it is not bad, but rather discontented and withered. I feel neither sick nor well.

You need not tell me again that the beginnings of all virtues are weak, that they acquire strength and firmness with time. I realise that those we show outwardly, such as greatness, a reputation for eloquence, or anything else which affects those who observe us, increase with time; but those that give us strength or make us seem more attractive need many years to be internalised through use over time. I fear that habit, which confirms things, entrenches these defects (or perhaps vices) more and more within me. A long presence in good or bad makes us resemble what we frequent.

I believe that my state of weakness can be likened to that produced when our thoughts jump between two opinions without choosing between good and evil. In a way, I am unsure of what is happening to me, so it is better to explain it to you so you can name my illness.

I confess that I have an exaggerated love of austerity. I like to live in my old house, I have no interest in four-poster beds or luxurious furniture, I feel at ease in my modest clothes, I enjoy the simple food I buy for myself, I am not a fan of strange hairstyles, nor jewellery; in short, I am satisfied with very little. I have to admit that I find houses with sea views in Mallorca, staying at nice hotels, or going to parties with famous actors appealing; and all of this makes me wonder which is better.

What's more, as you know, I try to be consistent, methodical and systematic in what I do. I don't like quick fixes, and I try to solve problems step by step. I like to have all the information on the table so that, with reflection and patience, I can find solutions. I try to be strict when it comes to following the rules, and I don't like to show my emotions in public. But, despite all this order in my life, at times I tend to think pretentiously and I let myself become arrogant, speaking with a mouth that seems not to be mine.

I have followed the commands of my teachers and participated fully in public life. It seemed right to take on responsibilities; not for my ego, which, as you know, is small, but to help friends and relatives and, in general, all citizens.

Whenever my spirit is struck by something to which it is not accustomed, as soon as some misfortune occurs, as happens to all other mortals, or when something does not progress easily as I expected, or when minor matters take up a great deal of my time, I try to return to my life of leisure. Just as tired and hungry cattle hasten their pace when returning to the farm, I hasten to retire and spend time within the walls of my house.

Unconsciously, my mind ruminates on these frequent misfortunes, and I think they explode in the form of malaise and dizziness in public, causing me restlessness in my public appearances.

I fear I am slowly breaking down and giving in to my instabilities, or worse; I feel as if I am always swaying, on the brink of falling. Yes, that is how I can best define my state, hence the fear of approving the habitual, what obscures our judgement. I think that many could have reached wisdom if they had not believed they were already there, if they had not hidden certain things within themselves and passed by others with their eyes closed. There is no reason to believe that the flattery of others is worse than one's own. Who dares to tell the truth? Who, surrounded by sycophants, as I am every day, is capable of no longer applauding themselves?

Therefore, I ask you if you have any remedy to tackle these doubts, to consider me worthy of owing you my peace. I am well aware that these variations in my spirit are not dangerous, but they cause me great anxiety. To use a nautical example to express what I lament, what distresses me is not the storm, but the seasickness. Free me, therefore, from this ailment, and help one who suffers with land in sight.

***

Seneca

I thank your dear mother for bringing me to you. The ways of letters are confusing and difficult, but she managed to make you love books.

I too have been quietly asking myself for some time what I could compare this condition of the spirit with, and I think that it could be better understood with an example: with the behaviour of those who, after a long and serious illness, are cured, but from time to time are afflicted with small complaints, become distressed, misinterpret any small problem with their body and go to the doctor. These people are not sick; rather, they are not used to health, meaning no vigorous action is needed to get back on the right path. Instead, we must have self-confidence, believe that our path is the right one and not to be seduced and lost amidst the footsteps of those who wander everywhere.

Do not let what you desire be shaken. It is something great; better still, it is sublime. I would call that state tranquillity.

So, what we are looking for is how to move

forward steadily, with gratitude towards yourself, feeling content with what you have around you and without becoming arrogant or depressed: this will be tranquillity.

First, let us take a general look at how to get there, then you can select what best suits you from the general remedy. First of all, we must reveal all vices, and then each person must acknowledge their part in them. You will understand to what extent your instabilities are less than those of your peers who are slaves to political positions, who, under the yoke of glittering names, are held back in their simulation more by shame than by will. The same applies to those who suffer from their lightness and continual changes of plans, always idealising what they have left behind, like those others who, being layabouts, do nothing more than yawn; add to this those who change from one side to the other, like those who have difficulty sleeping, until fatigue induces them to rest, living in such a way that they stopped not because they hate to move, but because of old age, the enemy of change. Also add to this those who do not cease to be inconsistent, not because of their steadfastness, but because of their apathy, and live not as they wish, but as they began. Innumerable are the forms of vice, but there is only one effect: being dissatisfied with oneself. And this is born of intemperance of spirit and cowardly or unprosperous desires when one does not get what one desires, or fails in one's efforts and relies entirely on hope.

Such people will always be unstable and changeable, the necessary consequences of those who live in uncertainty. They will use any means to reach their objectives, and will justify using dishonest means, in fact will oblige themselves to do so, meaning that when their efforts are unsuccessful, they are not saddened by what they have done, but by the fact that they have not succeeded. Then regret for what was plotted and panic about beginning something new takes hold of them and causes them a sort of disturbance with no escape, because they can neither command nor know how to obey their desires, because they cannot live the life they would wish for and their mind is paralysed by disappointment. Thus, all this is aggravated when they are forced into obligatory idleness, when they wish to maintain the entertainment that public life gives them, and not in their obligatory solitude, which cannot be borne by a spirit inclined towards public affairs, one that desires action and is tireless by nature, as, of course, it finds little solace in itself. In consequence, having abandoned the entertainment with which public life distracts those who move in it, they cannot bear their house, its walls, its solitude, and against their will they are left to themselves. Then comes weariness, that unease of a spirit that finds no rest, and this sad, weak resistance to forced idleness. When one is ashamed to confess the true causes of one's suffering, and this discretion leads to bottling up one's sufferings, the desires enclosed in such a small space are suffocated. And this is how melancholy and depression of spirit arise, as well as a thousand other fluctuations of the insecure mind, which lives on tenterhooks over hopes begun and saddened by failure.

That is the source of the state of mind of those who hate their loneliness, complain that they have nothing to do, and see the progress of others with the bitterest envy; sad apathy fosters resentment, and those who have not succeeded wish ruin on others. Rejection of the success of others and despair with one's own life produces a spirit irritated by one's lot. This leads to complaints about the times one has had to live through, hiding in corners, absorbed in misery, feeling sick and ashamed of oneself. The human mind is agile. It enjoys movement and anything that entertains and excites it.

And so they will plan random trips, change friendships, hobbies, cities, but they are always running away from themselves. But what good is running away? For many, death has been the result of this continuous change of plans that always ends in oneself and in a weariness of life.

You ask me: what is the remedy against this boredom? It would be best to keep busy in action and dedication to others. And this dedication can be carried out as you do, through politics, making yourself useful to your fellow citizens, or simply by collaborating, each one to the extent of his or her possibilities, like someone who collaborates altruistically and privately by teaching painting to children at weekends.

"Normal people," you say, "will hardly be safe amongst so many crazed, ambitious beasts who twist even the straightest words to get what they want, so sometimes I think the safest thing would be to withdraw from public life." If you devote the time you take away from your duties to your studies, you will not have abandoned your position, because when it comes to winning the fight, he who fights is just as important as the trainer who corrects and gives orders on how to face the rival; activities that may appear secondary, but are all part of the competition.

If you devote yourself to your studies, you will

have overcome the tedium of life and you will not wish for night to come so you can sleep, you will not find yourself tiresome or be unnecessary to others; you will have many friends and the best will come to you. If, on the other hand, we avoid any relationship with others and spend our lives only talking to ourselves, this confinement will be devoid of tasks and we will begin to waste time in a shameful way. Other than their age, older people often have no way of proving that they have lived.

Sometimes, I cannot deny it, we will have to withdraw; but we must do so with parsimony, thinking about how we can help our fellow citizens. If it is not possible to be president, serve as an example to other women in the world. If it is not possible to be a mother, help young mothers with no resources. Has silence been imposed on you? Help your fellow citizens with your muted advice. Are you not allowed to enter Parliament? Be a faithful friend, a good companion and a prudent guest in homes, at public performances, at parties. Therefore, remain in good spirits, do not limit yourself to your borders, but preach your good example in the world, which is your homeland. You will never find a closed door so big that you cannot find an even bigger one that is open to you.

What would happen if you no longer wanted to be in politics if it could not be as a leader of your country? Even if others occupy your current position and you have to collaborate in a secondary position, collaborate with your voice, with your advice, with your example, with your spirit; and if they cover your mouth, stand firm and help with your silence. The work of a good citizen is never useless; it is already beneficial just to see them, hear them, their gesture, their disposition, their step.

Why do you think that he who rests honestly is useless? Mixing leisure with business whenever any adversity appears or when public life is paralysed is, by far, the best course of action. Socrates was at ease among the tyrants and despots who put him to death: in a corrupt republic, the wise woman has the chance to show herself. In a prosperous one, insolence, envy and a thousand other cowardly vices reign. Therefore, depending on the situation, or on fortune, we will expand or shrink, but in any case we will move and not allow ourselves to be frozen by fear. It is better to be dead than to live as if you were dead; the greatest of all evils is to erase yourself from the list of the living before you die. So, if fate makes you abandon politics, set out at once for your leisure and your letters; as if you were sailing in a great storm, steer into port and free yourself from your burdens. Do not wait for circumstance to do it for you.

However, we must first analyse ourselves, then examine the work we are about to begin, and finally with whom and for whose benefit.

The most important thing is to examine oneself, because we usually believe we are capable of more than we are. Some are overconfident in their eloquence, others get into debt beyond their means. Others, with weak bodies, embark on exhausting tasks. For some, their shyness is not suited to public tasks that require shamelessness. For others, their stubborn pride makes them unsuitable for the courts. There are those who cannot control their rage and get angry to the point of saying reckless words at the slightest provocation, as well as those who do not know how to limit their quips and do not refrain from risky jokes. For all of these people, leisure is better than work.

Then we need to understand what we are going to undertake and compare whether our temperament is suitable for the tasks we are considering. He who pulls has to be able to handle what he is pulling; in fact, loads that are too heavy must be broken into smaller parts in order to be pulled. There are irrelevant issues that generate many others: these should be avoided. We should never embark on something from which we cannot freely withdraw; apply yourself to what you can finish, what you have the hope of finishing, and abandon those challenges that increase as you work on them, or do not end where you had hoped.

In all cases, we have to select people very carefully, to see if they are worthy of being part of our lives or if they deserve to waste our time and theirs, as some consider that we are indebted to them for services we did for them. Avoid those who try to repay their friends' help with gifts; they are trying to settle the account with donations. Nothing pleases the soul more than a faithful and pleasant friendship. How good it is when you share your secrets in complete safety, when their conversation eases your anxiety, their advice complements your plans, their enthusiasm dispels your sadness, and their very presence is a delight!

We will choose them, as far as possible, free of desire, because defects are contagious, and pass from one to the other simply through contact. Therefore, just as in an epidemic we keep away from those who are feverish and coughing, because we are in danger of contagion, so too must we try to select the least corrupt as our friends. But where do we find these perfect people? Let's select the least bad as the best. Above all, we must avoid those who are sad, who complain about everything, for whom there is nothing that is not a cause for lament. Although they may be loyal and affectionate to you, someone who protests about everything and is always anxious goes against peace.

Let us consider legacies, the main cause of human bitterness: if you compare all the other evils that torment us, such as illness, death, fear, regret, suffering, pain and toil, with the misery that money causes us, you will understand that it is wealth that will cause the greatest problems. Therefore, we must consider how much lighter a pain it is not to have it than to have it then lose it, meaning you must understand that the greater the poverty, the less we will have to lose, and the less torment we will suffer. You are wrong if you think that the rich are better able to bear ruin. The strong and the sick suffer the same pain from a wound; it does not bother those who are half bald any less than those with a full head of hair to have their hair plucked out.

As I have said, it is easier and more bearable to not accumulate property than to lose it, and for this reason you will see that those who have not been blessed by fortune are more joyful than those who have been abandoned by it. This is what I call peace. You might call it need, poverty or misery, or whatever other ignominious name you like, but think about the calm that comes from being surrounded by thieves, scammers or crooks when you know you are the only person they cannot harm, because they cannot take anything from you.

Do you think the man who counts his property, his investments, his capital, his income every day, and whose only concern is to know how much it has increased, is happy? I know we are not strong enough to give everything up, but let us at least reduce our needs so that we are less exposed to the onslaught of fortune. The bodies of men who fit the size of their shield are better suited to battle than those who are large, and whose parts protrude and expose them to wounds; the greatest wealth is that which pulls us back from poverty, but does not make us lose our heads.

We will agree with this measure of wealth if we appreciate frugality, without which there will never be enough money to satisfy us; especially when the remedy is in our own hands, because poverty can be turned into wealth by resorting to austerity. Let us get into the habit of avoiding ostentation, of assessing the value of things by their utility, not by their packaging or the attractive exteriors that adorn them. Let food appease hunger, let water quench thirst, let sexual pleasure be confined to the limits of what is necessary. Let us learn to live for ourselves, that our clothes and our food are not always dictated by the latest trend, but that we follow the customs of our elders. Let us learn to increase our continence, to repress lust, to temper pride, to placate wrath, to contemplate poverty without prejudice, to cultivate frugality, and, though many may be afraid to do so, to give our natural desires remedies obtained with little, to keep all undisciplined hopes and aspirations under lock and key, and to seek to obtain riches from ourselves, by our own efforts, and not from fortune.

We can never overcome the great variety of misfortunes that threaten us if we set sail in the midst of the storm; we must curtail our desires to prevent the arrows of fortune from reaching us. So, let us teach ourselves to dine without company, to be strict guardians of our property, to wear clothes that serve their original purpose, and to live in more austere houses. In the journey of life, just as in a race, we must take sharp turns.

Even when buying books, where money is better spent, it will be justifiable if you keep within certain limits. How can you excuse those who buy mahogany furniture or those who collect books by venerable talents while yawning through so many thousands of them, when the covers and titles please them more than any other part of the book? I would exonerate them now if they were really driven by an excessive fervour for knowledge, but not if these costly works of great geniuses are simply bought for display and to serve as wall decorations. Everything that is taken to excess is wrong.

However, suppose that you have entered into some difficult way of life, and, without knowing it, fortune has thrown you into a snare that you can neither undo nor break. Then, think that at first, those who are enchained endure the weight and chains, the impediments to their steps, with disgust. But afterwards, after deciding not to be angry at these burdens but instead to suffer them, necessity itself teaches them to bear the chains with strength, and habit teaches them to bear them with ease. At any moment in life, you will find distractions, diversions and delights that will make misfortune more bearable than loathsome. Knowing that we were born for hardship, nature has provided us with the ability to become accustomed to enduring calamity, and we soon become accustomed to the hardest instances. Nobody could withstand misfortune if it permanently exerted the same force as in the first blow.

We are all chained to fortune. For some the chain is loose and made of gold, while for others it is tight and rusty. But what is the difference? We are all in the same prison, even those who lock us up are themselves locked up – unless you think that a chain on the left hand is easier to carry than one on the right. Some are bound by their public position, others by wealth; some by lineage, others by humble birth; some obey the whims of others, others their own; some are detained in a strange place by work, others by leisure. Our whole lives are servitude. Let us become accustomed to ourselves, without complaining even a little, and let us embrace whatever good we have close by. There is no situation so bad that a balanced mind cannot find some benefit in it.

Do not envy those who, like you, stand at the top, for what appears to be a lofty height is nothing but a precipice. Those have been put in a predicament by a cruel destiny will be safer if they bring their pride, which has been swollen by the vanity of their office, to the same level as that of mere mortals. There will be others who want to cling to the summit of power, from which the only way to descend is falling head-first, meaning that they can prepare for a favourable fall with justice, clemency and kindness. Nothing will free us more from these fluctuations of spirit than to always mark some end to our success, and not let fortune choose when to end our careers, but rather to stop ourselves long beforehand. If we act in this way, although certain desires will stimulate our mood, they will not extend beyond what is controllable because they are finite.

These words of mine are addressed to the imperfect: he who fears death will never act as a living man, but he who is aware that his destiny was set the day he was conceived will live in accordance with what is stipulated, and with that strength of mind, nothing that happens to him will be unexpected. Because by understanding that he may experience the greatest misfortune, he disarms evil, which will not strike those who are expecting it and are prepared to receive it valiantly. Misfortune only severely strikes those who believe they are safe and think only of happiness. Illness, ruin, fire, accident, death: nothing is unexpected, I was aware that nature had embarked me on a troubled ship. Remember the times you have attended funerals, heard the heartbroken cries of parents, witnessed fires or comforted the sick:

"It can happen to anyone".

If one engraves these words deep within oneself, observes the misfortune that befalls others and remembers that there is nothing to prevent it happening to them, they will be prepared long before being struck. It is too late to prepare the spirit against danger after danger has already struck. "I never thought it would happen to me." But why shouldn't it? Where is the place where hunger and disease do not pursue the rich? Remember your city in the past where, in a short space of time, beauty and wealth turned to fire and destruction.

We must clearly understand that every situation can change and that what happens to others can happen to us, too. We must not arm adversity by not believing that anything could happen to us.

The next point is that we must not do useless work or work for useless motives, that is, we must never desire what we will not be able to achieve, nor, having achieved what we desire too late and after much work, discover the vanity of our effort. In other words, the work must have a result and the result must be worthy of the work, for sorrow comes from these two things: either from not triumphing in what we seek, or from feeling ashamed of having triumphed.

We must avoid the comings and goings that many practice, wandering through homes, businesses and markets, offering themselves to others and always acting like they are busy. If you ask any of them, even just as they are leaving their house, what they are going to do that day, they will tell you that they are going to work, yet they do not know what they are going to do for the rest of the day. They wander around looking for tasks, but they don't do what they planned to do at some point. Instead, they do what they found along the way. They move without meaning and without a plan, just like ants that climb a tree to reach the highest leaf and then descend to the ground, empty handed, without having obtained anything. Many people spend their lives in this way, which we can justifiably call active laziness. Therefore, all work should have a goal, and we must always keep that goal in sight. The restless are not restless because of work: they lost their minds because of false ideas. They do not set themselves in motion without expecting a reward in return: they get excited by the appearance of something and their crazy mind does not perceive its futility. He who wants to live a peaceful life should not do many superfluous things, in public nor in private. We should do not just many necessary things, but countless;

however, when our regular work demands it, it is better to remain still. You will agree that the more unnecessary things you do, the more you yield to the discretion of luck. It is wise not to tempt it often, but it is always better to remember its existence.

We must also make ourselves flexible and not become too attached to what we have set out to do. We must go where destiny takes us, not fearing change to our position or our lives as long as we do not fall prey to whim, which of all vices is the most hostile to rest. Stubbornness, of which fortune always takes something, needs to be anxious and miserable, but in the capricious, who is never repressed, it is something more serious. Both qualities are the enemies of rest. Neither wants to change anything, and both are dissatisfied with everything. The mind must be called to meditation; it tries to make the spirit retreat into itself, enjoy itself, admire its own work, avoid the goods of others as much as possible, feel devotion to itself, not to feel losses, and to experience misfortunes with dignity. The Stoic, Zeno, when he heard the news of a shipwreck in which all his goods had been lost, said to himself, "Fortune wants me to become a philosopher more quickly."

We gain nothing by scorning others' sources of

sorrow, because sometimes we ourselves are possessed by hatred of the whole human race. You realise how rare simplicity is, and how unheard-of innocence and frankness are, except for when it is for profit, and you remember the criminal victors, and the gains and losses of corruption; we see that ambition, unbridled by its just terms, shines with its very ineptitude, the spirit is hidden from the light, and the gloomy darkness emerges, as if good had been defeated. We must therefore try not to find people's vices odious, but rather ridiculous. We must remove the importance from everything and bear that which arrives with optimism: it is more natural to laugh at life than to be tormented by it. He who does not control his laughter shows more greatness of spirit than he who does not control his tears.

Let each of us think of all those things that make us joyful or sad, and you will see that what they used to say is true: that all people's affairs were alike in their principles, and there is nothing in their lives more divine than their own conception. Therefore, let us accept public morals and the vices of others calmly, without bursting into tears or laughter. Suffering for the suffering of others is an eternal misery, while taking pleasure in the misfortune of others is an inhuman pleasure, just as weeping and showing a miserable face when someone is burying their child is a useless sadness. Even within your own evils, it is fitting to give to sorrow only that part that it asks for, and not that which custom demands, because there are many who shed tears for the benefit of others, with their eyes dry when no one is looking at them, and consider it shameful not to weep when others do. We have already internalised this evil of being dependent on the opinion of others, to such an extent that we even feign grief, the simplest of emotions.

Now comes the part that, not without reason, is often the most saddening: when the best meet a bad end. Think of Socrates when he ended up dying in prison drinking hemlock. You will then complain that fortune has behaved so unjustly, and you will wonder what you can expect from life when the best meet the worst of fates. Cast your eye on the way they suffered; if they were strong, wish for their spirit, but if they went as cowards, nothing was lost. Let us laud those who deserve constant praise and say, 'The braver you are, the happier you are! You have already escaped from misfortune, from envy, from illness: you have already escaped from prison." Those who shun death when it is their turn and try to cling to life in any way must be scorned. We will never shed tears for those who die joyfully, nor for those who go weeping; the former took away my tears with his joy, and the latter, due to his own tears, does not deserve anyone to weep for him.

Another major cause of problems is not showing ourselves in a natural way and grooming ourselves to excess, as many people who live a life based on pretence and ostentation do. We must stop being tormented by the opinion of others, forget about those who undress us against our will, stop living behind a mask to disengage from the worry that distresses us, which is being surprised by an unexpected appearance. What a pleasure to live unadorned and in a sincere simplicity that shows us as we really are! However, let us exercise moderation in all of this: simplicity is not neglect.

It is also good for us to withdraw into ourselves assiduously, as dealing with others disrupts all that we had already composed, it stirs up passions where before there was calm, and aggravates the wounds of all that was badly healed. However, we should mix spending our lives alternately in solitude and in the crowd, because the former will awaken in us the desire to communicate to others, and the latter the desire to speak to ourselves, with one being the antidote to the other. Loneliness will cure us when we are sick of the crowd, and the crowd will cure us when we are sick with loneliness.

We should not keep continuous tension in our minds, but relax it with entertainment. Socrates was not ashamed to play with small children. He was even found on a broomstick, pretending to trot on a horse. The spirit must be given rest in order to regain its strength and return with more energy. Fields are left fallow for some time to later reap a better harvest; in the same way, we must free our minds from continuous effort in order to recover their strength after a brief period of rest and relief. A certain numbness and lethargy of spirit arises from continued effort. People would not be so attracted to this if play and entertainment did not hold a special attraction for them, although continued play takes strength and gravity out of the spirit; there is a lot of difference between easing something and letting it go entirely. Legislators established days off to encourage people to have fun. Some did this by taking days off every month, in other cases they divided their day between time for work and play. Others, for example, stopped receiving visits after the seventh hour in case a message might alter their mood and prevent them from enjoying the remainder of the day. We can even go so far as inebriation – not to drown ourselves, but for fun. It washes away problems, stirs the spirit and acts as a remedy for sadness and other ills. Just as moderation is healthy in the case of freedom, so it is with wine. It should not be done so often that the spirit adopts this bad habit, but from time to time we should lead it to freedom and merriment, disrupting our sad sobriety for a while.

With this you have, my dearest friend, the means to encourage peace and restore it. But you should know that none of these measures is enough for those who have to watch over something so weak if it does not have continuous, attentive care.

# III. TO THE INDOMITABLE

"Nobody will want to laugh at those who laugh
at themselves."

A llow me to write these notes to you as a
matter of urgency, after having witnessed
your appearance before the senators. You will be
worried about the outcome of the trial those
angry enemies are putting you through.
Therefore, I recommend that you listen to the
threats of your rivals without worry and, even if
your conscience inspires you with confidence,
wait for the most just sentence, but also be
prepared for the opposite to happen. Remember
your natural disposition, so you can act in
accordance with goodness, truth and justice.

Here are my tips for your appearance
tomorrow. These notes are taken from the past.
They are messy, tangled and perhaps excessive,

remembered and hastily compiled in the morning. I hope you find them useful. Reflect on them tonight and remember not to delay your rest, because tomorrow you will need to be at your best. I trust that they will serve as medicine to calm the unease that I believe afflicts you.

***

It is not without reason that I would venture to say, my friend, that between us and the other currents of wisdom there is the same difference as between women and men. Though both contribute equally to life, some contribute differently to others; some are born to lead and others to obey. The others are like bad doctors, who apply soft and weak medicines to the body, curing not as they should, but as they presume. However, we are the good doctors who do not care whether the remedy is pleasant, only that it heals the sufferer and leads us to the summit that cannot be reached even by the arrows of fate.

Some time ago, when I spoke to you about Socrates, you became indignant, you who revolts against injustice, that the century in which he lived had not come to know him, because he, who stood out amongst the best, had been put on the level of the mediocre, and it seemed to you shameful that in his last moments he should be received at the agora with spitting and other outrages befitting a crazed mob. Then I told you to be calm and to fear not, for the wise man can receive neither affront nor insult, and you must know that providence lent him to us as an example, as it gave us Ulysses or Hercules in the past, those who our people called wise men because they were undefeated in their labours, disdainful of delights, and conquerors of all dangers.

I remember when we spoke about these injustices and the sage's responses, you said to me angrily:

> These are the things that discredit your advice: you promise great solutions that not only cannot be desired, but not even believed. On the one hand, with great words you say that the wise man cannot be poor, but then you confess that he often lacks a place to eat and sleep; you affirm that he cannot be a lunatic, but you do not deny that he can lose his mind and say mad things; you affirm that he can never be a servant, but you do not deny that he must obey the commands of those above. So, at times I think you are a charlatan like all the others.

I suspect the same of what you say now, that the wise man cannot suffer insult; something which, if true, is very attractive. I think there is a big difference between not being insulted and not being outraged. It does not surprise me when you tell me that a wise man will bear insult in good spirits, because it is something that is acquired by receiving blows. But if you tell me that he cannot be wronged and that nobody is able to do such a thing to him, then I will leave everything behind, my life and my business, I will take my suitcase and go with you.

My objective was not to adorn the wise man with words alone, but to elevate him to a place where insult cannot reach him. So, will there never be anyone who provokes him, who tries to harm him? There is nothing so sacred in nature that nobody would attempt to commit sacrilege against it. Invulnerable is not he who has never been attacked, but he who has not been wounded; therefore, you will know and I will show you the wise man. Can it be doubted that the strength of he who has never been vanquished after enduring countless onslaughts is less than that of he who has never been attacked? You must know that the wise man will be better even after he has remained unaffected by outrage, than if no outrage has been done to him. And it is he whose efforts do not bend, and who is not alarmed by the violence of his enemies, that I will call hardworking, not he who wastes his leisure time amongst the indolent. What I want to tell you, and forgive me if all this is too dense to read tonight, is that the wise man is not offended by any insult. It does not matter if many stones are thrown at him, they do not affect him because he is made of iron. Do you think that when that stupid Persian king who appears in *300* darkened the sky with arrows, trying to subdue the Spartans and conquer Greece, any arrows reached the sun? Just as what is sacred escapes the hand of man, and no harm is done to the gods when temples are destroyed or their statues melted, so when the wise are attacked with malice and insolence, it is in vain. "But it would be better if nobody tried to do such things," you said. You were wishing for something difficult: that mankind would be inoffensive, and that there would be no evil. Not committing such acts is to the advantage of those who want to commit them, not those who will not be affected by them even after they have been committed. What's more, perhaps the power of wisdom is best shown by calm in the midst of provocation, just as an armed general's greatest show of strength is calm in enemy lands.

Now, if you like, let us distinguish between outrage and offence. The first is by its nature more serious. The second is less important, and only bothers the thin-skinned. It does not injure us, only aggrieves us. So great is the weakness of the human mind that it believes there is nothing more bitter than insult. We have reached such extremes of stupidity that we suffer not only from pain, but also from the idea of pain, like children who are frightened of the dark, of deformed faces, and who burst into tears at the sound of strange names, banging doors and the like, all caused by their disarmed ignorance.

The goal of outrage is to cause harm to the person; but wisdom leaves no place for it to enter, because for wisdom there is no evil but indecency, which has no place where once virtue and honesty have entered, by which it is shown that insult cannot reach the wise man. Because if suffering some evil is what is known as insult, and the wise man does not suffer, it is evident that insult has nothing to do with him, as every insult is a certain diminution of the subject into which it falls. It is not possible to receive it without some loss, whether to the body, to dignity or in any of the things that are outside of us. The wise man, however, cannot lose anything, because he has everything deposited within himself and has left nothing to chance. All his possessions are in a safe place and he contents himself with virtue, which needs no luck. And so it can neither increase nor diminish, for what has reached the top can rise no higher, and fate can only take away only what it has given. And as it did not give virtue, it cannot take it away; it is free, inviolable, firm, uncontrollable, and so fortified against events that not only can it not be overcome, it cannot even be bent.

I know that you will think about it again tonight, after the previous paragraph, about how this sage of whom I speak does not exist and how this is all just empty talk. I do not invent him as the glory of the human race, but I show him as he has been exposed to us at times, and always at long intervals, as in the case of Socrates in antiquity or, closer to us, let us take the example of Saint Teresa of Calcutta.

Think also that outrage will emerge from all those things that expose us to danger, such as a bribed accuser, a false accusation, as is happening to you today, or provoking the powerful to be against us. It is also an insult to take from a person their earnings or prizes that were obtained with great effort over much time, or the favour of an important client from whom they have received great benefits. The wise man, who does not know how to live by hope or fear alone, flees from all this.

I heard how this morning you were called an accomplice, weak, how your character was mocked, and at one point I saw how the colour of your face changed. We will talk about that later.

As we have already dealt with the first part of our subject, now let us move onto the second, in which we will use argumentation to prove that the wise man cannot be offended. Offence is less important than insult, which we can complain about rather than seek revenge for, and which the courts would not consider worthy of punishment. This passion is moved by the weakness of spirit that shrinks from a word or deed that is unworthy of it, such as "he has not taken my words into account", "he never greets me when I arrive" or "he has said indecent words to me" and other similar things, which I would call the complaints of a fussy spirit. These matters mainly affect the well-off and the unhappy, because those who have real troubles have no time to waste on fictitious evils. Due to excessive idleness, naturally weak temperaments are moved by events that are most often misinterpretations of reality on the part of he who interprets them. As such, this shows that there is no sense or self-confidence in he who feels wronged by an offence; he considers himself to have been slighted, and this feeling causes a certain humiliation of spirit, which shrinks and becomes depressed. However, no one can offend the wise man. He knows his greatness, he gives himself the assurance that no one has the power to offend him, and not only does he overcome these things (which I call annoyances of the spirit, not miseries), he does not even feel them. There are, however, other matters that do strike the wise man but do not destroy him, such as physical pain or illness, the ruin of his city during a catastrophe or the loss of children and friends. I do not mean to say that the wise man does not feel these things. He is made of neither steel nor stone. The wise man does receive certain blows, but he heals them, bandages them, and represses them; when it comes to lesser matters, he does not even feel them, nor does he employ his accustomed strength in enduring evils against them. Instead, he does not even consider them, or smiles at them.

Bear in mind that insults come mostly from the proud, the arrogant and those who are burdened with a sick prosperity, and the wise man possesses the weapon with which to defeat this conceited passion, the most beautiful of all virtues: magnanimity. And armed with magnanimity, insults will harm us as much as falling off a horse in a dream. Think of children who bite and hit their parents and utter foul words; we consider none of this an offence. And why? Because those who commit the act are incapable of slighting us.

The same disposition of spirit that we have towards children, the wise man has towards those whose childhood continues beyond their youth. Or has age brought any benefits to those who have the same defects as children, but increased by time? When they differ from children only by the larger size of their bodies, but are no less capricious, unstable, eager for immediate pleasure, fearful and harmless not because of their natural disposition, but because of fear? Therefore, these people cannot be said to differ from children in any way. While children covet sweets and gifts, these adults are greedy for delicacies and gold; children build pretend houses out of sand on beaches while the adults build walls and roofs as if they were doing something important, turning what was intended as protection for the body into danger.

But why were you reluctant to accept the wise man's steadfastness when you can observe the same thing in others, but with a different motive?

Does the doctor get angry with the deranged? Just as the doctor endures indecent words when he amputates a patient's limb, so the wise man will listen to insolence, but knowing that those who are overdressed, salubrious and well-groomed are not healthy, he will see them as disobedient patients and treat them. This means that if the wise man does not accept the greeting of a beggar or if the worst-dressed of the citizens does not show him veneration, he does not consider it an offence. Likewise, he will disregard the rebuffs and remain unaffected by the conceit of the rich, because he knows that they are no different to the poor. In fact, they are more miserable, because the poor need very little and the rich need a lot. Consequently, he will not be moved by anyone's offence. If he were ever affected by an insult or an offence, he would lose his calm, which is an asset that belongs to him. And he will never give those who vilify him the pleasure of seeing that he is aggrieved, because, naturally, he who is disturbed by the scorn of others loses his calm and also loses the ability to disregard, which so bothers those who offend.

What is this so-called offence? Some have laughed at my ears, some at my baldness, some at the way I walk and some at my short stature, but what is insulting about stating what everyone can see? If only one person says it, we laugh, but if we hear it in the presence of more people we become indignant, and we do not allow others the privilege of saying the things we say to ourselves. So, let us steal the weapons from the insolent, let us anticipate and start laughing at ourselves. Nobody will want to laugh at those who laugh at themselves.

He adds that it is a certain kind of revenge to take the enjoyment of the offence away from the person who committed it, as they usually say, "Poor me! I don't think he understood it." The fruit of the insult is in the fact that it is felt, and in the indignation of the offended party.

Despite the offences, we must stay away from conflict and fighting. We must flee far from them; all the provocations of the ignorant must be scorned, holding the flatteries and the offences of the people in equal esteem. We must neither rejoice nor grieve over either of them. Otherwise, out of fear of insults or out of spite, we would omit many things and we would turn away from important work and services due to the anguish of perhaps hearing something that would hurt us. Sometimes, being indignant towards the powerful will show our feelings freely. And if we think that freedom means not suffering something, we have been deceived; freedom is having a mind that soars above outrage, makes oneself the source from which joy springs and separates oneself from the external causes that make us live our lives enslaved by the fear of the laughter and tongues of others.

So, if anyone can offend, is there anyone who will not be offended at some point? The wise man and the aspirant will use different remedies for this. Those whose education is not yet complete and who behave in accordance with public opinion should bear in mind that they will spend their lives on the receiving end of outrage and offence; everything will be more bearable if they are prepared.

The greater your responsibilities or wealth, the more energetically you must resist, remembering that the strongest always fight on the front line. When you receive insults, affronts, harsh words, or other slights, bear them as you do distant voices, as lightning bolts that you hear and see from the window of your house; and though they may strike and annoy you, do not yield to the impetus of the enemy, but defend the position that nature signalled to you. And if you ask me what this position is, I will answer: that of the human being.

The wise man's help is different to yours. While you continue to battle, he has long been victorious. Do not fight against your own good, foster this hope in your spirit, gladly receive what is best and affirm: in the republic of mankind there is one who is invincible and who is not ruled by chance.

I very much hope that these notes can lighten your spirits for your appearance tomorrow.

# IV. TO THE PHILANTHROPIST

"It is not that we don't have enough time, it is that we waste it."

M ost mortals, dear friend, complain bitterly about the malevolence of nature, because we are born to live for a scarce time, and even the time we are granted runs so fast and so quickly that, with very few exceptions, we depart just as we are preparing to enjoy it.

This does not happen only to unaware or ignorant people, who lament this universal evil, but illustrious people have also had this calamity befall them. Hence the famous quote from the greatest of doctors: "Art is long, but life is short." It is not that we don't have enough time, it is that we waste it. Life is by far long enough to achieve the highest of goals if the time we are gifted is well spent. But when it is squandered on luxury and indifference, when it is offered to no good, when in our last will we claim it, we understand that it has fled without us realising it. This means we do not receive a short life, but we make it short. We are not short of days, but we waste them. Just as the greatest wealth can be squandered in months by a bad manager, yet increases through use in the hands of a good manager, so life is long enough for those who manage it well.

Why do we complain about nature? She has been kind to us. Life is long if you know how to use it. Some are possessed by an insatiable avarice, others by a laborious diligence in doing arduous, useless tasks; one devoted to wine, another paralysed by laziness; some, possessed by the greed of merchants, travel the world in search of wealth; many have been kept occupied by pursuing the fortunes of others or complaining of their own; there are those who live their lives in voluntary slavery to their superiors or their work; many pursue no clear goals; inconsistent and unsatisfied, they change their plans when faced with any novelty; some have no principles to guide them, but fate will take them off-guard, between laughter and yawns. It is certain to happen, and you will remember the words of the greatest poet when he said as a prophecy, "The part of life that we really live is short." The rest of our existence is not life, it is simply time.

Vices besiege and surround us from every side. They do not let us lift up our eyes to see the truth, but instead keep us prostrate and chained to our passions. Their victims are not free to return to themselves; if at any time they break free, they will be shaken, and will find no rest. Do you think I speak only of the unfortunate who suffer ills? Look at those who are surrounded by people because of their prosperity: they are suffocated by their possessions. For how many is wealth a burden? How many turn pale because of their constant pleasures? How many people do not have enough time for themselves because of their multitude of clients? Look through them all, from the least to the greatest: one is looking for a lawyer, others for clients to sell to, the other for an answer to a call: all are servants to everyone, but none is their own master. Some will show senseless indignation, and will bitterly complain of the insolence of their superiors for not having had time to attend to them when they were asked, as if they had a right to complain about another's pride when they have no time to attend to themselves.

I wish I could call one of the oldest ones and tell him:

I see that you have reached the limits of human life, you are over a hundred years old or even more. Come, call your life and let's settle the accounts. Tell us how much of your time you spent with your boss, how much with your friend, how much arguing with your partner, how much dealing with clients, how much travelling from one side of the city to the other for work. Add to that how much time you have spent sick due to your own fault, how much time engrossed in idleness; you will see that you have not lived as many years as you believed you had.

Look back and remember when you steadfastly pursued your purpose, how many days you have spent as planned, when you have done what you wanted to do, when your face showed its natural expression, when your mind was unperturbed, which of your labours will last, how many were taking away your life without you realising what was happening, how much useless sorrow, foolish joy, greedy desire have taken away; how little of yourself is left. You will realise that you die before your time.

What is the reason for all this? People live as if they were going to live forever. They do not reflect on their fragility or on the time they have already lived. They waste time as if it were infinite, not realising that perhaps this conversation, this minute, this word, could be the last. They have all the fears of mortals, yet all the desires of immortals. You will have heard many people say, "When I turn sixty, I'm going to retire so I can enjoy life." Who guarantees you will get there? Aren't you afraid of wanting to enjoy scraps of life at the end? Isn't it strange to postpone the start of your life to the moment it is ending? What a foolish neglect of our mortality it is to procrastinate the start of our lives.

You will find that the most powerful people say they yearn for leisure, that they acclaim it and prefer it over any of the other pleasures they enjoy. Sometimes they wish to descend safely from their pedestal but, even if nothing shakes them from the outside, their fortune falls of its own accord.

Caesar Augustus never stopped asking for rest and relief from the troubles of public life, and he used to end all his conversations with this sweet (if unrealistic) lie with which he consoled himself: that one day he would be able to live for himself. In a letter he wrote, "These desires are better promised than realised, knowing that the joyful reality is still far away, I already enjoy the pleasure of words." So desirable was leisure to him that he enjoyed it in advance in his thoughts.

Amongst the worst, I will count those who devote their time to wine and lust; no one is more shamefully occupied. The others, though seduced by an empty image of glory, lose themselves, although with a certain dignity. Even if you quote to me the greedy, the furious, those who provoke unjust confrontations, they are nothing more than people who err as people. But those immersed in wine and desire are unworthy. Examine these people's time; consider how many hours they spend on calculations, how much on engineering deception, how much feeling fear, how much wooing, how much on their own and others' quarrels, how much on preparing parties, which for them is already an obligation, and you will see how their desires and their fears leave them no time to breathe.

Finally, all agree that nothing, neither eloquence nor liberal work, can be done adequately by one who is permanently occupied, for the mind, when it is occupied with many minor matters, is not able to focus on anything serious, and everything new that enters it is expelled as though it were a foreign body. Nobody knows less about life than the busy: there is nothing more difficult to learn. Of the other arts there are masters everywhere. In contrast, it takes a lifetime to learn how to live and, perhaps more surprisingly, it takes a lifetime to learn how to die. Great people have renounced all their power, all their riches and pleasures for the sole purpose of learning to live, even at the end of their days. Many of them left us lamenting that they had not yet learned; how much less will the busy know.

Believe me, not allowing anyone to steal your time belongs to great and lofty spirits that rise above weakness, and therefore their lives will be very long, because all their time belongs to them. They will leave no moment idle or unoccupied. No-one will be left under the control of others; they have found nothing worth trading their time for. Therefore, they will see that it will be available to them, as opposed to those from whom it has been stolen and who will have very little of it.

And there is no reason to believe that these people are not aware of their fault. You will hear many of those who are overwhelmed by great prosperity lament amongst the crowd of their clients, or amongst their lawyers, or amongst their other honourable miseries, "I can't go on living like this." Why can't you? All those who come close to you push you away. How many days did work take from you? How many a suitor? How many politicians seeking favours? How many powerful friends who keep you around not for friendship, but for ostentation? I beg you to count the days of your life, and you will see how few and useless they have been to you.

He who reached the presidency he so longed for wants to leave it behind and says, "When will this year be over?" The other, who is in charge of the festivities and who felt so lucky to have received the order, laments, "When will this end?" Everyone rushes through life, working with desire for the future and weariness of the present. But to he who makes the most of his time, who plans each day as if it were his last, who neither longs for nor fears tomorrow, what new pleasure can a new hour bring? Everything is known and enjoyed ad nauseam. You can dispose of your fortune at will: your life is safe. Something can be added to it, but not taken away. The same thing happens as to the body, which, being full and satisfied, accepts some food, but without having felt like eating it. There is no reason for you to think that a person with wrinkles or grey hair has lived too long; they have not lived long, they have existed long.

I find it strange when I see people asking for time from others, and these others give it to them happily. Both fix their eyes on the object for which time has been requested, but neither on time itself; as if what was requested were nothing, as if what was given were nothing. People play with the most precious commodity in the world because it is intangible, it is immaterial, it is invisible, and therefore they do not value it. People receive their wages with gratitude and in return rent out their labour, their services and their effort. Nobody values time. They use it generously as if it were a gift. But when they fall sick and see the possibility of death approaching, you will see these very people kneel down and weep before the doctors. They do not hesitate to sell all their possessions in order to live, so great is the inconsistency of their feelings. If everyone could see how many days they have left to live, how alarmed they would be to know how few they are! How they would make the most of them! It is easy to administer what you know, no matter how small, but that which you do not know when you will lose it must be cared for more jealously. There is no reason to think that such people are unaware of the importance of time, many even offer to give part of their years to those they love. And they give it to them without knowing what they are giving, though the result is that they lose it without increase to the recipient, but they do not realise the loss. The loss of something unknown to them is imperceptible. No one will return your years to you. Life will continue on its way and never turn back or review its course, it will make no sound, it will not remind you of its swiftness or its sweetness. It will slip away in silence. As it began on the first day, so it will flow. It will not turn back, it will not stop. And what will the result be? You were distracted. Life went by. In the meantime, death will present itself and, whether you want to or not, you will have to face it.

Is there anything more foolish than the sentiment of those who flaunt their prudence? They live with much suffering and effort in the hope of living better; they waste their lives on wanting to live. They plan for the distant future, when procrastination is life's greatest error: it cancels out the day they are living and tears them away from the present in the hope of a better future. The greatest difficulty in living is waiting, because it wastes the present and depends on tomorrow. You leave to the hands of fortune what is in your own hands. Where are you looking? How far are you expanding? All that is to come is uncertain: *carpe diem*.

Remember these words: "The best days of miserable men are the first to fly away."

Why do you hesitate? If you do not hold onto your days, they will fly away. Even if you believe you are grasping them tightly, they will fly away. Therefore, you must use them as fast as you can to counteract their transience and drink them as from an abundant stream that will soon run dry. Why, then, do you wait impassively for long years of prosperity when time runs so fickle and so fast? Is there any doubt that the best days of busy people are the first to flee? Old age surprises them when they are still children, and they arrive there defenceless, without expecting it. They did not realise that they had been on their way, day by day. In the same way that a traveller reads during a journey and, without realising it, arrives at the destination without expecting it, busy people only realise what life is about at the end.

Let us divide life into three periods: what was, what is and what will be. Of these, the present is brief; the future, uncertain; and the past, certain.

The past is the only period to which fortune has lost its rights, the only one that cannot be changed. But the busy have lost it. They have no time to remember, and even when they can, they avoid it so as not to remember what they regret. No one, unless every one of his actions has always been controlled by his own conscience, willingly remembers the past. He who has coveted ambitiously, scorned proudly, squandered recklessly or betrayed disloyally must necessarily fear his own memory. That is our sacred and untouchable part, the part beyond human misfortune. It is beyond the dominion of fortune and is imperturbable to desire, fear and disease. It can never be shaken or beaten; we will possess it forever, unfadingly.

The present is uncertain, changeable; yet the past, when you claim it, will present itself and you will examine it, something for which the frivolously busy have no time. It is the privilege of calm and serene minds to be able to reflect on all the stages of their lives, but the minds of the busy are like animals under the yoke; they cannot turn and look back.

The present is very short. In fact, for some it seems not to exist, it is always in motion; it flows, runs and disappears before it arrives. Busy people are preoccupied with the present. It is so short that it cannot be grasped, and even for those who are busy with so many tasks, it slips away. You may ask me who I mean when I say "busy people". It is not only those who go door to door seeking customers from dawn, nor those who night finds in their work, nor those who you see glorious, always surrounded by their followers. Even the leisure of some people is a chore; in their villa, in their armchair, on their bicycle, in complete solitude, even if they have cut themselves off from the whole of society, they bother themselves. Or would it be better to say that these people do not live in leisure, but rather that their occupation is laziness? Do you call someone who collects coins and cleans them every day idle? Someone who lists and checks their assets every day? Someone who spends all day at the barber's, checking the new hairs that are sprouting, or complaining that barber did not shave above his ears? How angry such people get with the barber if he is careless, as if he were styling a man! Who amongst them would not prefer the State to decay before their hairstyle? How many of them care more about their hair than their health? Who would not prefer appearance to honour? They do not have an idle life, but a lazy trade.

It would take time to describe the lives of those who waste the whole day playing sport, sunbathing or playing cards; they will not be idle if their pleasures turn into work.

Idle men will also be those who give themselves to wisdom; only they truly live. Not only do they enjoy their time, but they also add to it; all time spent belongs to them. Unless we are the most ungrateful creatures in the world, we should recognise that our ancestors, the founders of the schools of thought, were born for us and they prepared the way for us. Through their efforts, the most beautiful things have been brought out of obscurity and shown to us; we have access to any age, we can enter wherever we wish, and, if we desire, we can pass through the narrow limits of human weaknesses using our minds, and expand into a great number of ages at will. We can argue with Socrates, learn with Aristotle, calm ourselves with Plutarch, liberate ourselves with Nietzsche, subdue man's nature with the Stoics, exceed it with the Cynics, or transgress it with your contemporaries, such as with García Márquez, and delight in a blizzard of petals falling from the ground towards the blue sky in summer in Colombia. If nature allows us to become friends with any era, why not set aside this miserable space of current time and surrender to the past, which is eternal, without borders, and live alongside the best? They will always be available. After visiting them you will feel happier than when entering, and you can find them night or day. They will not force you to die, they will teach you to die. None of them will consume your years, but they will give you theirs. You will take from them everything that you want. You will have friends to seek advice from, from whom to hear truth without insult, who will praise you without flattery, and who you can imitate.

We often say that it is not in our power to choose our parents, that they are given to us by chance. But we can still be reborn and become the children of whoever we want. There are houses of noble intellect – choose which one you wish to be adopted by. You will inherit not only the name, but even the property, which you will not need to hold onto greedily: the more you share it, the bigger it will become. They will show you the way to immortality and will raise you to heights from which nobody will be able to topple you.

Those who forget the past, neglect the present and fear the future have a sad and short life; when they reach the end, the unhappy realise too late that they were busy doing nothing.

So, dear friend, leave your business and get away from the crowd; you have sailed through many a storm, now head for a calm port. Think how many waves you have faced, how many storms you have endured in your personal and professional life. You have long shown your virtue in adversity: now see how you respond in leisure. You have given most of your life to your business, now take some of your time and dedicate it to yourself. I do not summon you to lazy or careless inaction, nor to extinguish all your energy with vulgar pleasures; this is not rest. You will find tasks to spend your energy on, to occupy yourself calmly and happily, helping others.

# V. TO THE LEGEND

"Happy is he who is not a slave to his fears and desires."

I look forward to being able to meet you again at the end of summer, when I will answer many of the questions you have asked me in your previous letters, but for now I will offer you my thoughts and advice.

My last few days in Corsica have been spent reading and enjoying the presence of some mutual friends whose company I had been deprived of due to my current situation. I am not enough for myself and I need your contact.

When you arrive in the city, do not forget to go to the pillars of the Temple of the Dioscuri to make offerings. They will give you the power to overcome your rivals, and to navigate between them calmly in the midst of the storm.

***

Everyone, dear friend, wants to live happily, but they are lost when it comes to finding what makes life happy. It is so difficult to attain that the more energetically it is pursued, the further one will get from it if one takes a wrong turn along the way.

We must first define what we are seeking, and then define how to reach it as quickly as possible. Along the way, if it is the right path, we will see day by day how much progress we have made and how close we are to the goal towards which our natural desire pushes us.

As long as we keep on lurching, following no guidance but only the cries and clamour of those who invite us to continue erring in various directions, we will waste our short life wandering, even if we devote ourselves day and night to good understanding. Therefore, once we have decided where we are going and by which road, let us not start the journey without the advice of an expert who has previously explored the region we are heading to, because this journey is not subject to the same conditions as others. Normally, following the marked paths and asking the locals guarantees that the destination will be reached, but here the most worn and frequented roads are those that will leave us the most lost.

There is nothing more important, therefore,

than not to follow the flock of those who have gone before us like sheep, and not to go where people go, but instead where we should go.

Now, nothing will get us into greater trouble than submitting common opinion and believing that what everyone else regards as such is better, taking falsehoods as true things, and living not according to reason, but according to imitation. That is the cause of the large herd of people running around and charging at one another. In such an agglomeration, when the crowd presses upon itself, no-one can fall without dragging down the person next to them, and the person who goes first causes the destruction of the one behind. You can see this in real life. Nobody simply errs by themselves, but rather one is the cause and example of the error of others. It is dangerous to follow the lead of those who go before us, and as it is easier to believe than to form our own opinion, we never reflect on life. We perish because we follow the examples of others who lead us to ruin. We will be cured of this evil the moment we disengage ourselves from the crowd, but we must be careful, because the crowd will fight against reason in defence of its own error.

First, look at what Aristotle considered happiness to be:

Whether one considers happiness to be virtuous good deeds, financial independence, a stable and pleasant life, or an excess of things and persons, with the power to preserve and enjoy them, many people confess that some or many of these things are happiness.

These words from one of the greats deserve credit, but while they were correct at the time, I think today they need some correction. So as not to keep you going round in circles, I will give you my opinion of what a happy life is: it is one that suits its own nature. This cannot take place unless it first takes place in a sound mind, one that remains sound over time. Next, it must be bold and vigorous, bearing all circumstances with commendable courage, adapted to the times in which one lives, careful with the body and its vicissitudes, but not with excessive care. He must also value the things that adorn our lives, without overestimating any of them, and he must be able to enjoy the gifts of fortune without becoming a slave to it.

You will understand that peace and freedom will reach us when we put away all those things that excite or frighten us; instead of sensual pleasures and fears, always causes of slavery, we will gain an immense, immutable and stable joy, along with peace, calm and greatness of spirit, and kindness, because all cruelty is a sign of weakness.

Therefore, the definition of our supreme good can be expressed in a long and diffuse form, or written in a short and concise form. It would be the same if we were to say that "the greatest good is a mind that scorns the accidents of fortune and is content with virtue" or "an unconquerable strength of spirit, well acquainted with its surroundings, chivalrous in its deeds, showing courtesy and consideration for fellow citizens".

If you will accept another definition from me, we could say he who neither fears nor desires thanks to reason is happy; but stones do not feel fear or sadness, nor do cows. He who does not understand what happiness is cannot be called happy. Put those whose ignorance of themselves and their obtuse nature reduces them to the level of cattle in the same bag. There is no difference between one and the other. The former has no understanding, and the latter has only a corrupted version of it, twisted and cunning only for their own misfortune. The happy life is immovable and is based on true and reliable discernment. A happy person is the one who can correctly judge all things. Happy is the person who is satisfied with the conditions of their life, whatever the conditions may be; the one who submits all circumstances to reason.

Some deny that pleasure and virtue can be separated. I do not see how these two such distant elements can have any interconnection between them. If they were inseparable, we would not see pleasant but not honourable things, and other honourable things only achieved after great suffering. Add to this that pleasure sometimes reaches corrupt people, yet virtue does not admit them; you will even find people who are sad in pleasure, because of the very pleasure that corrupts them. None of this would happen if pleasure was connected to virtue. Virtue is something lofty, sublime, regal, unconquerable, tireless, while pleasure is helpless, servile, base, perishable; its hideouts and homes are the brothel and the tavern. You will find virtue in schools, market squares, village houses, covered in dust, burned by the sun, with hot hands. You will find pleasure hidden out of sight, looking for dark corners in public bathrooms, enclosures and places that fear the visits of order, soft, weak, reeking of wine and perfume, pale or perhaps painted and made up with cosmetics.

That is why our ancestors recommended following the best life (not the most pleasurable one), in which pleasure is not the guide, but the companion of an upright and moderate mind.

Although virtue may bring us pleasure, we do not seek it for that reason; it is not the end towards which it works, but it procures it for us as a gift. In the same way that some flowers might sprout by chance and brighten our eyes in a field ploughed to plant wheat, although the object of the work was not to admire the flowers, but to seek sustenance, so the pleasures of life are not the reward or the cause of virtue, but will come as an added bonus.

Anyone who thinks that happiness consists of lazy leisure and alternations of gluttony and lasciviousness, when he believes that his vices are in accordance with the rules, will not indulge them in solitude and in secret, but will indulge himself in the light of day.

I repeat that no one can live in pleasure if they cannot also live honestly, and you will understand that this is not the case with irrational animals, who measure their happiness in proportion to their food. Again, I affirm that what I call a pleasant life cannot exist without the addition of virtue. Now, who does not know that idiots do not drink from these sources of pleasure, or that vice is full of joy, or that the mind itself suggests depraved variants of pleasure? In the first place, arrogance, excessive self-esteem, haughtiness over others, blind devotion to their own interests, dissolute luxury, excessive exaltation motivated by the most insignificant and infantile causes, and also the causticity that takes pleasure in insulting others, the indolence and decadence of a dull mind, apathetic with itself.

All of this dissipates with virtue, which pulls us by the ear and evaluates pleasures before using them and gives no greater importance to those it has tried, it simply permits their use, and its joy is not due to their use, but to moderation in their employment. However, when moderation diminishes pleasure, it spoils what for some is the highest good. You are captive to pleasures, I subject them; you give yourself to pleasure, I use it; you think it is the supreme good, I do not even think it is good; you would do anything for the sake of pleasure, I do nothing.

It is senseless (and ignorant of our own condition) to complain because we have not obtained something, or because obtaining it was arduous, or to be surprised or indignant at those evils that befall both good and bad men, such as disease, death, suffering or any other accident of human life. Let us accept with magnanimity what providence wants us to bear. We are all bound by this oath: to endure the evils of a mortal life and to accept with grace that which is inevitable. We were born into a monarchy: our freedom obeys destiny.

Those who bark at us once again say what they always do:

> Why then do you preach what you do not follow? Why do you control your words in front of your superiors and consider money indispensable, and are worried when you lose money, or cry when you hear about the death of your wife or a friend? Why do you pay attention to rumours and feel annoyed by slander? Why is your garden more manicured than necessary? Why don't you dine according to your predicaments? Why is your furniture so excessive? Why are you drinking wine older than you are? Why do you show off your jewellery? Why do you plant trees that will give you nothing but shade? Why does your wife wear jewels hanging from her ears that are worth more than your friends' houses? Why do your children wear such expensive clothes to school?

To these you can add, if you wish, the questions "Why do you have a second house near the sea?" and "Why do you have more than you need?" I will add more reproaches in the future and blame myself for more things than you can imagine, but now I will answer:

> I am not a wise man and – I will add, to increase his resentment – I never will be. I am not required to be at the level of the best, only to be better than the worst. I will be happy if every day I diminish some of my vices and correct my faults. I have not reached perfection and it is clear to me that I will never get there. Compared to his crippled feet, I am an Olympic champion. I say this not only for myself, who am hooked on all kinds of vices, but for those who have made some progress.

"You talk one way and live another," objected the wicked creatures who showed the bitterest hatred of the best, like Plato, the one who preached how we should live, not how he managed to live, trying to silence the racket of his vices every day. Use his life as an example of moderation at moments when you are overwhelmed.

We must admire those who attempt such great challenges, even if they fall.

Who can doubt that a wise person, if he is rich, will find it easier to develop his virtue than if he is poor, in the latter case being able only to show that he is not crushed or perverted by his poverty, while if he is rich he will be able to show his disposition for temperance, generosity and greatness.

Put me in the house of someone very rich, where even the most insignificant things emit luxury. I will not inflate myself for the riches of that house of mine, for they do not form part of me. Take me under a bridge to live amongst the homeless, I will not look down on myself for sitting amidst those who stretch out their hands for alms. What does it matter if those who cannot escape death are lacking a piece of bread? Well? I prefer a life of luxury to living under a bridge. Remember where you came from, dear friend, and where you are now.

I would like each day to transpire in accordance with my wishes, new joys to be linked with the previous ones; even so, I would not be proud of myself. Change all that fortune to disgrace, let my spirit be distracted by loss, sorrow, different attacks; let every hour suffer different disputes, even so, attacked by great miseries, I shall not consider myself the most miserable of beings, I shall not curse any particular day, because I took care not to have bad days. So, what is happening with all of this? I would rather hold onto my joys than repress my sorrows.

I will scorn the rule of fortune, but given the choice, I would choose the best of it. I will turn what comes to me into something good, but it is clear that I prefer everything that happens to me to be pleasant and enjoyable, and not to cause me discomfort. We should not expect any virtue to exist without work. Some virtues need encouragement, but others require rather some restraint. Just as we hold back our bodies on a downward path or push them up a steep one, so the paths of some virtues go uphill, while others go downhill. Can it be doubted that patience, courage, perseverance and all the other virtues that have to face strong opposition, and crush fortune under their feet, are climbing, fighting, tiring with every step forward they take? Why?! Is it not equally evident that generosity, moderation and affability slide comfortably downhill? The latter we must keep in our spirit, lest it flee with us. First, we must encourage and stimulate it. Therefore, we must apply these energetic and combative virtues to poverty, and the more sparing, light ones, those that barely support their own weight, to riches. This is the difference between them, but I would rather deal with those that I can practice calmly than those whose practice involves blood and sweat.

"What difference is there, then, between me, who is at times a fool, perhaps because of my youth, and you, who is wise?" you ask. An enormous difference: riches are slaves in a wise man's house, but they are rulers in a fool's.

# VI. TO THE ARROGANT

"The great remedy for anger is time."

You have urged me, dear friend, to prescribe you some means of subduing anger, and I understand from your experience that you fear this dark and angry passion more than any other. All other passions have some peace and tranquillity; this one consists only of commotion, rage, resentment. It lacks concern for oneself for the sake of harming the other, hungry for revenge, which will bring with it an avenger.

Some wise people have indicated that anger was a brief madness, as control is lost, decency is forgotten, relationships are disregarded, the sufferer becomes obsessed with what he wants, closes himself off from reality, becomes agitated without reason, and is unable to discern what is just and true; reason collapses like a building falling into ruins and rubble.

By their expressions, you will see that those possessed with anger are not sane. Just as the symptoms of insanity may be seen in an unabashed and threatening expression, the sad face, the changed colour, the quickened walk, the restless hands, the hurried breathing, so you will see the irascible with the same symptoms: their eyes are inflamed and burning, their faces redden from the blood boiling in their veins, their lips tremble, their teeth grind, their hair ruffles and stands on end, their breathing is forced and noisy, their joints creak as they writhe, their speech is slurred and unintelligible, they clap their hands repeatedly... This is the terrible appearance of those who are deranged by anger.

You can hide and nurture all other passions in secret, but anger emerges to the exterior and shows itself in gestures, becoming more evident as it grows furiously. Think about how animals behave moments before they attack: they go from calm to ferocious. The boar foams at the mouth and sharpens its tusks by rubbing them together, bulls charge at the air and paw their hooves against the ground, lions roar, snakes swell their necks when threatened and rabid dogs show their teeth. No animal is more frightening than when overcome by fear. I am aware, of course, that there are other passions that are difficult to hide, such as fear and desire, which show signs and make themselves known in advance, changing, for example, the expression on our faces. What is the difference then? These passions are visible, but anger explodes.

Now, if you want to know the damage, no affliction has cost mankind more: children sold into slavery, slaughter, poisoning, cities razed to the ground, nations wiped off the map...

Now that it is clear what anger is, the difference between anger and irritability seems clear, in the same way that being tipsy is different from being drunk, or being scared is not the same as being terrified. The irritated individual may not be angry, just as the angry individual may sometimes not be irritated.

There are some forms of anger that are extinguished by shouting, some that are frequent and difficult to manage, some that are violent and no friend to words, some that spill out in a torrent of curses; some forms go no further than sulking and profanities, but others are deep, heavy and remain within. There are hundreds of possibilities within this thousand-faceted vice.

We have therefore already defined what anger is, how it differs from irritation, and in what forms it presents itself. Now let us look at whether it is natural, whether it is useful, and if it may be of use to any extent.

If it is in accordance with nature, we will notice it if we observe people closely. Who is more inclined towards love for others than human beings? On the other hand, what is crueller than anger? People were born to help; anger was born to destroy. People seek to come together; anger seeks to drive them apart. We seek to be useful; anger, to harm. We want to help the needy; anger, to attack even those closest to us. Anger, as we said, is hungry for punishment, and the presence of this evil in people's peaceful hearts is not at all in accordance with nature.

Sometimes punishment will be necessary, but it will be without anger and with the use of reason in order not to harm, and to heal with the appearance of harm. When doctors are faced with mild illnesses, they first thing they prescribe is food, rest and exercise in order to rebuild health simply through consistency. Thus, they hope that moderation will do the body good. If there is no improvement, they will withdraw something; if the patient still does not respond, they will reduce the food and, if there is no improvement, they will start with more severe drugs and treatments, even amputating a limb if necessary. No treatment that heals can be considered harsh.

You ask, "Would it be possible to use anger,

although it is not natural, because it has been useful at some point? It lifts the spirits and stirs them against the worst dangers." This is why many think that it is better to control anger, not to eliminate it, to reduce it to healthy limits by removing its excesses, retaining those elements that do not weaken action and do not turn the spirit foolish.

Firstly, it is easier to keep vices out than to try and control them once they have been let in, because once they have become masters, they are more powerful than their owner, and will not tolerate reduction or mutilation. Moreover, reason, which is in command, can only rule if it is not connected to the passions; once contaminated by them, it can no longer contain that which it should have refused entry. Certain things are under control as long as they are not shaken and remain still, but once movement starts they can no longer be stopped. We are swept away and there is no turning back. Those who plunge from the top of a building can offer no resistance to the irrevocable fall of their body. They cannot avoid – nor regret – the result of what they should not have begun. In the same way, if the mind is delivered to anger or other passions, it will no longer be able to contain the propulsion or weight, and it will inevitably be drawn into the depths of vice. Without doubt, the best thing to do is reject the first signs of anger, extinguish the first sparks and try hard not to fall into it. Ultimately, there is nothing useful about anger.

You state, "Anger is necessary, nothing can be achieved without it. It fills the soul and nourishes the spirit, but it must be used as a foot soldier, not a general." This is false. If it listens to reason and follows its guidance, it is no longer anger, which has rebellion as its main characteristic. Consequently, reason will never enlist violent and unforeseen impulses over which it has no authority and which it cannot subdue except by opposing similar ones, such as fear to anger, anger to laziness or desire to fear. Let virtue always be kept far from evil. May it never have to take refuge in vice. A spirit in such a state, defended by its own evils, unable to be strong unless it is irritated, or active except when greedy, or calm except when fearful, will find no rest and will be agitated and wavering. He must live as a slave to every passion that befalls him.

You say, "Good people anger when their family and friends are wronged." Because many people become angry when their relatives suffer badly, do you think that people believe that what they do should be done, because almost everyone justifies the passions they recognise in themselves? But they do the same if their drink is not cold enough when it arrives, if someone breaks a glass in their presence, or if their shoes are splashed with mud. They are not moved to anger by virtue, but instead by weakness, like children who mourn the loss of a parent as much as the loss of a toy. Getting angry on behalf of your loved ones is not a sign of affection, but rather of weakness. The right thing to do is to defend children, parents, friends or neighbours with responsibility, by choice, with intention and prudence, not out of impulse and rage. Since no passion craves revenge more than anger, for that very reason it is incapable of revenge. Impetuous and naive, like any other form of greed, it stumbles in the pursuit of what it seeks. Furthermore, we should not regard vices as a good thing just because they have been in some way beneficial in the past; fever helps to heal some diseases, yet this does not make it desirable. It is a terrible cure that puts health at the mercy of illness. Likewise, anger, like poison, a fall from up high or a shipwreck, will not be considered beneficial, even if it was at some point beneficial to us, because it has mostly proved to be detrimental.

"Anger," you say, "is useful because it makes us

more violent." Therefore, inebriation should be considered in the same way, as it makes us violent and defiant, and many believe they are at their best when they are drunk. By the same logic, one might think that outbursts and madness are necessary for strength, as madness often makes us more impetuous. "Has not the fear of death roused even the most battle-shy?" But anger, drunkenness, fear and other similar solutions are useless and disgusting stimuli, which do not strengthen virtue, which need nothing that vice can deliver, and only cheer indolent and despicable minds. No one is braver as a result of anger, except he who would not be brave at all without it.

Again, you insist, "It is impossible for a good man not to become irritated by evil." According to this logic, the better one is, the more inclined to anger one should be. But don't you think the opposite is true? A good man will be calmer, freer from passions and will not hate anybody. Why, then, should those who err be hated, as it is error that drives them to such faults? A prudent person does not hate those who stray, otherwise he would have to hate himself. Look back at all the times you have acted inappropriately and contrary to custom, how many behaviours require forgiveness, and you will see that you should be irritated by yourself. A fair judge will not change his sentence depending on whether he is judging another or himself. I declare, there is no-one who can absolve himself, and he who declares himself innocent will not take into consideration his own conscience, but will use vice as his witness.

Reason is balanced and listens to the parties at the hearing. It gives itself time to find the truth step by step, while anger is hasty. Reason wants its actions to be just, anger wants its actions to appear just. Reason only considers the facts at hand, anger is distracted by extraneous facts. An assured countenance, a firm voice, free speech, sober dress and the affection of the people inflame anger. Countless are the times it condemns the accused because it hates the lawyer; though it has the truth before its eyes, it loves and protects error, it refuses to be convinced, and, once an action has begun badly, it considers stubbornness more honourable than modesty in recognising the ruling.

So far, we have talked about the usefulness of anger and whether any part of it or its effects could be used. The subject was plentiful and easy to handle, but now we will be moving into more arid areas. Now, the question is whether anger arises from reason or from impulse, that is, whether it acts of its own accord or if, like the other passions that flourish within us, it happens without our knowledge. There is no doubt that anger arises from the appearance of a received offence, but the question now is whether anger flourishes without the assistance of reason, immediately following the appearance of the offence, or whether it begins with the help of reason. Anger can do nothing without the approval of reason, for to conceive the idea of offence and to aspire to revenge, and to unite these two elements – that we should not be offended and that it is our responsibility to avenge offences – cannot be a mere impulse that is excited without our consent. Impulse is a simple fact, but reason is complex and composed of various elements. The person understands something that has happened, they become indignant, condemn it and take revenge; all of this cannot be done without the consent of reason.

You say, "Where is this question coming from?" We need to know what anger is. If it arises in spite of us, it will never listen to reason, because all movements that exist against our will are uncontrollable and unavoidable, like shivering when we bathe in cold water or drawing back when certain parts of us are touched.

Our hair stands on end when we receive bad news, our face reddens at indecent words, we get dizzy when we look down from great heights: it is not in our power to avoid any of these things, no reason can prevent them from happening. But anger is dissipated by reason, as it is a voluntary defect of reason. It is not one of those defects that belong to the human condition and which, therefore, can befall even the wisest. We must count the agitation of the soul when it remembers an offence amongst them. We feel the same emotion when we see a performance, hear the news or read about past events. We are affected by the sight of children going hungry while their rulers swim in abundance; sometimes we get worked up because of music or images of torture and death, both of which affect our reason; hence we laugh when others laugh, we are saddened by the sorrows of those close to us, and we are elated by the victories of certain athletes. All these feelings are not anger, nor are they fear, just as when we witness the collapse of a building in a performance or when we read about the siege and subsequent slaughter of the soldiers at a fort in the past. They are emotions of minds that are reluctant to be excited. They are not passions, but they do indicate that they could become passions.

None of those impressions which happen to

influence reason deserve to be called passions, as it suffers them rather than provokes them. Passion, therefore, does not consist of being afflicted by impressions, but rather of surrendering to them and continuing their indications. Consequently, if someone imagines that pallor, weeping, excessive blinking, sighing or the like are signs of passions, he is mistaken, and does not understand that they are mere impulses of the body. Thus, the bravest person turns pale before a tribunal, the legs of the boldest soldier briefly tremble when the battle signal is given, the general's heart leaps out of his chest when the lines come face to face, and the hands of the most eloquent orator freeze and tingle just before he begins his speech. Someone may consider themselves wronged and desire revenge, but for some reason will be persuaded to abandon their intention and calm down. This, therefore, is not anger. It is an emotion of the spirit under the control of reason.

When you see the theatre packed with a crowd, the Capitol overrun with people, or the stadium crammed with a rabble, you can be sure that there will be more vices than people amongst them. There is no peace amongst those you see well-dressed. Any one of them will try to ruin another for a small benefit; the benefits will come from the offence of another. They hate the fortunate and scorn the unfortunate; they bear the powerful with disgust, yet oppress the weak. They are ignited with different desires and will destroy anything for a little pleasure or loot. They live as if they were in a gladiator school where the people who live there must fight one another. It is a society of wild beasts but, unlike beasts, which are docile amongst themselves and refrain from biting their own kind, people tear each other to pieces. They differ from animals above all in that animals are docile and do not bite the hand that feeds them, whereas people rage against those who support them.

Anger, therefore, should never become a habit, but sometimes we will feign anger to arouse the slumbering minds of those we address, like prodding a horse to incite it to move. We will sometimes frighten those who will not listen to reason; but being angry is as useless as being sad or afraid.

And so? Aren't there situations in which anger arises in us? Yes, but in these moments, more than ever, we must confront it. Look at boxers. They take blows to weaken the opponent, and do not strike when anger commands them to do so, but when opportunity invites it. It is said that the best coaches teach their pupils not to get angry, as anger spoils their science and they only think about how to harm, not how to win. Reason counsels patience, but anger incites revenge, and those who have overcome initial evils expose themselves to still greater evils. Knowing this, Muhammad Ali tried to ignite this passion in his rivals so they would abandon reason and he would be able to overcome them more easily, which he achieved with Joe Frazier.

Having discussed what anger is all about, let us move on to how to remedy it. There are, in my opinion, two remedies: the first is preventing ourselves from falling into anger, and the second is preventing ourselves from doing wrong once we are angry. Just as we sometimes follow a regime to keep our bodies healthy, or sometimes apply medicine to it when health has been lost, we will do the same with anger, which we must either chase away or placate. To bypass it, certain general rules of conduct must be impressed upon us. They can be divided into those that need to be stamped during young people's upbringing and those that are applied in adulthood.

Education should be carried out with the greatest care, for it is easy to mould minds while they are tender, but difficult to eradicate vices that have taken root within us.

It is the greatest service to devote ourselves to

children's complete education, even though it is a difficult task. It is our responsibility to take care not to nurture anger in them, nor to dull their spirit. This needs special attention, as both opposites, both that which needs to be enlivened and that which needs to be extinguished, must be nurtured in the same way, and even the most attentive can be deceived by their similarity. Children's spirits grow with freedom and wane with servitude; they increase when they are praised and they are led to expect great things of themselves. However, the same treatment produces arrogance and insolence, which means we must guide them between these two extremes. Let nothing degrading or servile be tolerated, let them not beg for anything or be granted anything for doing so. Let what they receive be for them, for their good behaviour in the past or for promises of good conduct in the future. We will not let them become irritated in competitions with their peers. We will teach them to maintain friendships with those they compete with so they learn that the important thing is not to wound, but to vanquish. On the occasions they emerge as victors or do something remarkable, let them enjoy the victory, but do not let them show it too much, because joy leads to conceit, which in turn leads to exaggerated and excessive self-esteem.

We will give them some rest, but without corrupting them into idleness and indolence, and we will keep them away from luxuries, because nothing makes children more prone to anger than a childhood that is soft with excess. Children spoiled with excess more often fall into anger. He who was never denied anything, whose anxious parents wiped away tears against the advice of their elders, will not be capable of bearing any offence.

Can you not see, my friend, that greater fortune is followed by greater anger? This is especially seen in those who are rich, noble, or placed in great positions, when prosperity has taken the emptiest and most trivial passions from their minds. Prosperity feeds anger when the proud man's ears are bestowed with flattery by sycophants who tell him, "He has answered you! You don't act in accordance with your dignity, you underestimate yourself." Even sound and well-educated minds will find this and other similar things difficult to bear. Flattery, therefore, should be kept away from children. Let them hear the truth, even if they sometimes fear it. Let them stand up in the presence of their elders. Let them receive nothing in anger: let them receive in peace what they demanded with tears. Let them observe the riches of their parents, but not enjoy them. Let them receive reproach for bad actions.

Once, a boy who was brought up in Plato's house saw his father shouting passionately when he came home, and said, "I have never seen anyone shout like that in Plato's house." I have no doubt that this child will sooner imitate his father than Plato. Above all, their food should be frugal and their clothes should be simple, like those of their classmates.

These precepts apply to our children; in us, the accident of birth and our education no longer admit error or advice. We must contend with what follows. Let us face the first cause of anger: the belief that we have been wronged, which we will not accept easily. We must not become angry even when the insult is manifest, because some false things have the appearance of truth. Let time pass, because time reveals the truth. Let us not open our ears to slander, let us be on our guard against such weakness, let us know that we are not willing to believe what we are not willing to hear, and that we will not become irritated before forming an opinion. What more can I say?

We get angry not only because of slander, but also because of suspicion; a glance or a smile makes us irritated at innocents because of false interpretation. We should, therefore, plead the absentee's cause against oneself and keep anger in suspense, because a delayed punishment may be applied later, but one already imposed cannot be reversed.

Believing what we hear causes great evil; we should often not listen, because sometimes it is better to be deceived than to be suspicious. It is good to free our spirit from suspicion and mistrust, as these are the causes of anger. "That man greeted me rudely", "So-and-so didn't want me to hug him", "What's his name cut me off when I started to talk", "So-and-so didn't invite me to his party", "He gave me a dirty look"... There will always be excuses for suspicion. What we need is simplicity and a benevolent interpretation of reality. We must not believe anything until the truth is forced upon us, and we must vehemently reproach ourselves every time we have erred in judgement so that we do not fall back into the same trap.

Another consequence of the above is that we should not get angry about small and insignificant things. It is simply madness to lose control because our food was served cold, because the cutlery is dirty, because it is raining heavily, because we are late for an appointment or because the neighbour's cat comes into our garden. Nothing feeds anger more than excessive and unsatisfactory excesses; the spirit must be hardened so that it feels only the most severe blows.

If we are to be impartial judges of what happens, we must persuade ourselves that none of us is blameless. This is where our greatest indignation comes from: "It's not my fault", "I did nothing wrong"... Instead, declare that you do not recognise that you have done wrong. We become indignant when we are punished, even if we are making a mistake at that very moment, adding insolence and obstinacy to our offence. Who can say they have never broken the law? Even if such a person exists, what poor innocence it would be to always follow the rules of the law. Our obligations go beyond the letter of the law! How many things do generosity, kindness, honour or justice urge us to do that are not inscribed in the law? We are not able to comply with the narrowest interpretation of innocence: we committed evil, thought evil, wished evil and incited evil. We remained innocent because the desired evil did not succeed. After thinking about this, let us be fairer towards those who are lacking, and let us not become angry with the good. Because if we are angry with them, what will we do to others? And even less so with providence, because all the inconvenience that befalls us follows the laws of life; disease may strike us, true, but somehow we must flee from this fragile home that was handed to us.

You will hear others say that someone spoke ill of you. Think about whether you spoke ill of them first, and reflect: how many people have you spoken ill of? Let us suppose that some do not mean to do us harm, but return the evil received from us, that others act with good intentions, others out of obligation, others out of ignorance, and even those who do it on purpose do not always do it with the intention of offending, because they may have been led to offend by the attraction of saying something witty or because there was no other way for their gain.

He who remembers how often he has been the victim of false suspicions, how often fortune has assisted him and he has done his work by feigning evil, how many persons he started off hating and ended up loving, will refrain from being so quick to anger, especially if he says to himself after hearing the offence: "I have done the same." But where will you find an impartial judge?

He who desires the wives of his friends, considering that being a couple is a reason for desire, he himself does not tolerate anyone looking at his own partner; nobody demands more fidelity than the betrayer, nobody demands more truth than the liar, nobody demands more justice than the slanderer. We always have the vices of others in plain sight while our own seem to be hidden behind our backs. Hence, a lascivious father reproaches his son for endless partying and disapproves of the slightest hint of lust in others, even though he has gone beyond all the boundaries of vice. And so dictators become furious towards murderers, thieves are irritated by those who rob temples, and modern politicians, as you well know, my friend, appear to be angered by the corruption of others.

Most people are not angry at sins, but at sinners. As for us, we will be more moderate if we ask ourselves: "Have we ever committed a similar offence? Have we ever made that mistake? Should we condemn such behaviour?"

The great remedy for anger is time: call for delay at first, not to forgive the offence, but to judge it. If it is delayed, it fades away. Do not try to confront it immediately, because its fierceness is retained. Attack its parts and it will be defeated. We get angry about things we hear from others or things we have seen or heard ourselves. Now, we should not rush to believe the things that affect us. Many lie to deceive us and others because they themselves have been deceived. Some try to win our favour by making false accusations and inventing injuries they have suffered just to appear angry with us. There are those who cheat out of spite and seek to break up close friendships. There is also the suspicious person, who likes confrontation and wants to watch the confrontation he himself ignited from a safe distance.

If you were to pass judgement in a trial, even for a small amount of money under dispute, you would not take anything for granted without evidence and witnesses. You would let both sides speak, you would give them time, you would not dispatch the proceedings in one day, because the truth is revealed after hearing all parties. And do you condemn your friend without evidence? Do you become indignant with him before you hear him, before you analyse his words, before you know who is accusing him or what the charges are? Have you listened to both parties? He who instigates against your friend will remain silent if he has to prove his words. He will say, "If you find me out, I will deny everything I have said, I will say no more." At the same time, you are pressured and he withdraws from the dispute. He who speaks to you only in secret will never speak to you in truth.

We are witnesses to some offences. In such cases, let us examine the disposition and purpose of those who commit them. Perhaps it is a child. Then let us forgive his youth. He does not know that what he is doing is wrong. He may be a father. He has rendered such great services that he reserves the right to wound. Perhaps she is your wife. She has made a mistake, just as you make mistakes. He could be a judge. He considers his opinion to be right, and yours wrong. It could be a king. If he punishes the guilty, praise him, because he is just; if he punishes the innocent, praise him, for he is powerful. Perhaps it is a calamity or an illness: it will affect you less if you endure it calmly. Think now that perhaps he is an imbecile. If you become angry at him, you will be his equal.

We have said that there are two ways of getting angry. The first is when we believe we have been offended, which we have already discussed, and the second is when we believe we have been treated unfairly, which we will tackle now. People feel that some things are unfair, some people feel they should not have to suffer them, and some people did not expect them. We judge every fortuitous evil to be unjust, and therefore we are especially exalted against that which is against our will or expectations, and therefore we are irritated by domestic trifles and call the indifference of those close to us an offence.

How, then, do the offences of our enemies affect us? Because we did not expect them, or at least not on such a large scale. This is due to our excessive self-esteem; we believe we are untouchable, even to our enemies. Every person has the spirit of a despot within him; he is ready to commit excess, but not to suffer it. Thus, it is ignorance or arrogance that drives us to anger. What is so strange about an enemy doing us harm? Remember that there is no worse excuse for a ruler than to say, "I didn't think of it". Think about and expect everything.

"Anger contains a certain pleasure, as it is pleasing to return the harm received." No, it is not honest to repay evil with evil. Great souls are characterised by scorning offence. The most cutting form of revenge is to consider the adversary unworthy of it. Great is he who serenely listens to the barking of small dogs.

You say, "We will be treated with greater respect if we avenge our offences." If revenge is to be used as a remedy, let it be done without anger, and not for pleasure, but for utility. It was often better to pretend not to have received it than to avenge it. The offences of the powerful must not only be borne with composure, but also with a cheerful countenance. They will repeat the offence if they believe they have already imposed it. The worst thing about spirits that have been made arrogant by fortune is that they hate those they offend. Everyone knows the words of that courtier of despots when someone asked him how he had achieved the rare honour of growing old at court and he replied, "Receiving offence and giving thanks for it." Sometimes it is better to acknowledge offences than to avenge them.

Offended by the clothes and hairstyles of Pastor's son, a distinguished Roman gentleman, Julius Caesar sent him to prison. When the father begged for his son to suffer no harm, Caesar, as if the plea had made him reconsider the penalty, had him put to death and, to soften the brutality for the father, invited him to dinner that evening. Pastor came with a serene countenance, showing no grief whatsoever. Caesar made a toast to his health and posted a guard to watch over him. The wretched man took the cup, feeling that he was drinking the blood of his own son. The Emperor sent him perfumes and garlands of flowers and sent people to observe whether he used them: he did. On the very day he buried his son or, rather, the day he could not bury him, he was seated amongst one hundred guests at Caesar's banquet, and, old and gout-riddled as he was, he drank so much that he could hardly stand, without shedding a tear, without allowing his grief to betray him by showing the smallest sign; he dined as if his plea had successfully obtained his son's pardon. And you ask me why he did all this? Because he had another son.

Therefore, we must refrain from anger, no matter whether it is provoked by an equal, a superior or an inferior. A confrontation with equals is uncertain; with a superior, madness; and with an inferior, despicable. It is a wretched and miserable person who responds to blows with blows. Ants and mice bare their teeth when you move your hand towards them, as do the weak, who believe they will be harmed if you touch them. If someone becomes irritated with you, please them with attention; a fight only takes place if both confront one another.

# VII. TO THE VIRTUOUS

"The debt to be paid for being born is having to be useful to others."

You ask me, "Why does everyone recommend vice to us? Can't we withdraw and look for an example of someone's life that we can imitate and that will allow us to live happily?" This can only be achieved in leisure, where we can live according to the best, where nobody, with the help of the masses, will disturb us or interfere with our still weak judgement. Only with leisure will life, which we waste on superfluous activities, flow according to nature. In fact, the worst of our evils is that we continually change our vices, because we lose the advantage of being able to extinguish our habitual vices. We seek pleasure in vice, and are disturbed by the fact that our decisions are not only swift, but also erroneous. We fluctuate back and forth, grasping at one thing after another; we let go of what we desired a short while ago and try to recover what we let go, oscillating between desire and remorse. We depend entirely on the opinions of others, and it is that, what many people praise and wish for (not what deserves to be praised or wished for) that we consider best. We do not assess whether the path is good or bad, we only appreciate it because of the number of footprints that advance along it, without taking into account that there are none from anyone who has returned.

You will say,

> But what do you say now? You had told me in the past that I should remain active until the end of my days, that I should participate in public life, that I should never stop working for society, that I should help private people, that when I grow old I should help even my enemies. You maintained that I should keep myself from leisure until death, and that, if circumstances permitted, I should even shun leisure while I was dying. Why this change now?

Now I will prove to you that I am not deserting my mentors, no more than they deserted theirs, though I would be excused if I followed their example rather than their commands. I will divide what I am going to tell you into two parts: firstly, that from childhood, a person can give themselves entirely to contemplating truth and, secondly, that once they have reached old age and are weary, they have every right to apply themselves to others.

Think of the possibility of there being two States, one public and great, in which gods and men exist, its only borders being what the sun does not touch; and the other, in which we have been deposited by the accident of our birth, as yours may be, in America. Some serve both States, the major and minor, at the same time; others serve only the minor, others only the major. We can serve the greatest even in leisure. In fact, it is even better to serve in leisure, investigating what virtue means and whether it is one or several, whether it is nature or art or music that makes men good, whether everything contained within the earth and sea is unique; whether the universe is infinite and immortal or doomed to contract and belongs to the class of finite things. What service is it to providence to contemplate all this? Let there be witnesses who can share such beauty.

We often say that the greatest good is to live in accordance with nature. It conceived us for both purposes: for contemplation and for action. Let us now prove what we said before. Who will not take this for granted if after studying himself he does not recognise the great interest he has in discovering the unknown? How our curiosity is ignited by any kind of story or adventure!

Some undertake long journeys and experience the fatigue of long journeys for the simple reward of discovering something hidden and remote. This is what draws people to performances, what leads them to rummage around in what has been closed off, to pry into the secret, to unearth the ancient and take an interest in the customs of distant peoples. Nature has granted us an inclination towards curiosity, and knowing her beauty and goodness, she has engendered us to be spectators of her vast work, because if she only showed things so grand, so noble, so sublime to solitude, she would lose the fruit of her efforts. So, you can be sure that she wanted to be truly contemplated, not just briefly looked at. Look at where she placed us: she sat us in front of her, naked, and let us gaze upon her without blushing. She allowed us to follow the course of the stars from their rising to their setting; she arranged six constellations by night and six by day, and displayed herself before our eyes so as to excite our curiosity to discover the rest of the stars.

We have not yet observed all things, nor do we

know their true extent, but it has awakened in us an interest to find out, and it lays the foundations from which our knowledge can pass from the obvious to the less known, and ascertain something older than the world itself, such as the origin of the stars: what was the state of the universe before those elements were separated from the primeval mass? What principle dissociated them? Who assigned things to their places? Is it according to nature that the heavy should sink and the light float, and whether behind the weight of bodies there is some higher force governing them? Our thinking goes beyond the walls of heaven, and is not content with knowing only what is shown to us.

But, you say, it is different if you dedicate yourself to contemplating nature without expecting anything in return, just for the pleasure of observing it, as if I spent whole afternoons watching and learning how butterflies flutter amidst the flowers. In that case it would be very attractive, and I think pleasant for me, but difficult to perform these days, to be able to break with all my work and what I have achieved so far, all that effort. I don't know if I would be able to. I would lose it all.

To that I reply,

> With what intention do you dedicate yourself to music, if you never rest and never set aside time to take your mind out of the daily frenzy you endure, and your natural spirit already seems to miss your mind? It is by no means advisable to devote oneself to the accumulation of wealth by abandoning virtue, and to do nothing except work hard without exercising intellect. All these things must be combined and united with one other; just as how virtue in leisure without action is an incomplete and weak good, as it does not share what it has learnt with others. What is the wise man's aim when he withdraws into leisure? He knows that in leisure and in action he can be of service to posterity.

I told you, "You must intervene in public affairs unless something impedes you." If the state is so corrupt that it is beyond help, the intelligent person will not work in vain or waste his strength on fruitless efforts. If he has already lost influence or strength, and if the State refuses his help and his health is no longer with him, he should no more undertake a trip for which he is not prepared than a ship with broken sails should take to the sea, or a blind man enlist in the army.

If the State we dream of cannot be found on earth, it is clear that leisure is necessary for everyone, because the best alternative to leisure is not available to us.

If one says that sailing is a wonderful thing, but then goes on to say that it is not advisable to sail in areas with frequent shipwrecks and where storms are common and lead pilots astray, I imagine that this man, while praising sailing, is forbidding setting sail.

Therefore, he who still has health and fortune has the right, before any storm thwarts him, to keep himself safe, and to offer himself to the noble arts and leisure, and to the service of those virtues that can be practised even by the most isolated. The debt to pay for having been born is having to be useful to others; if possible, to most of them, and if not to all, at least to a few; if not to the few, at least to our neighbours; and failing all that, at least to ourselves. By helping others, we fulfil our obligation to humanity. Just as he who makes himself worse not only harms himself, but harms those whom he could have helped if he were better (for he who seeks good for himself seeks it for others), so he who seeks to be better will do good to others by the fact that he is preparing that which will be of service to them.

# VIII. TO THE EXEMPLARY

"He who is not content with what he has, even if he thinks he owns the whole world, will be unhappy."

Seneca

In June I will visit your city once again. You say that passion invades its streets in that month. Lust also invaded Rome during the solstice festivals, formerly in honour of Juno, and the enormous preparations made everything animated. But today there is no longer any distinction between work days and festival days; and those who said that June used to be a month, but that nowadays the whole year is lived, were right. I will return the first week of August with the intention of arriving in Rome for the offerings at the Altar of Hercules, under the Basilica of Santa Maria in Cosmedin, which I would like you to attend. In the past we sacrificed a bull to honour Hercules for having freed us from Cacus, a tradition that you still maintain, but it seems that in your case, Hercules has succumbed to Bacchus. My family will participate in this year's ceremony and torchlight procession, where I would like you to join us.

You ask me about poverty and how a lack of goods affects the spirit. You will understand that honest poverty is something joyful, and that, being joyful, it is not poverty. Only he who understands this well is rich, and it is not only he who has little who is poor, but he who desires the most. The greedy man has little use for what he has locked up in his house, or the amount of property and people who work for him, if he still desires that which is not his own and his mind is not on what he has, but on what he covets. You asked me what is the term of wealth. The first is having what is necessary and the second is possessing enough. There is nobody who can enjoy a peaceful life while they are only concerned with increasing their capital, and nothing will benefit the owner unless he is prepared to lose everything.

In accordance with nature, one who enjoys a compound poverty is considered rich, for he is content when he does not suffer hunger, thirst or cold. And to achieve this, you don't have to bow down before the powerful, search in faraway places, or be born the child of a deity, because you can easily find what nature asks for.

We sweat for the superfluous and useless, and this is what makes us consume our lives in vain hopes and stray from our path. Because it is easy to find enough to live. He who understands poverty and is content with honest moderation is rich. He who is not content with what he has, even if he thinks he owns the whole world, will be unhappy. If you live in accordance with the laws of nature, you will never be poor. If you live according to opinion, you will never be rich. Good deeds enhance the spirit, riches bring insolence.

Nothing belongs more to man than not having what he may desire; in your body there is little to take, for no one will shed your blood just to see it flow; the thief ignores the poor passenger, who will find safety even on dangerous roads. I do not discourage you from holding onto your possessions, but you should possess them without suspicion, which you will do if you realise that you can live without them and if you receive them as transient things, turning away from those who seek you out not for who you are, but for what you have. Poverty is to be loved, because it shows you who really loves you.

*\*\**

Warren

I am grateful for the invitation, and I will certainly honour you with my presence during the celebrations in Rome.

Thank you for your words. I share them entirely and they are of great help to me, because they confirm my thoughts. In addition, I would also add a phrase that I often repeat, but it seems that many do not understand (or do not want to understand): "Everything I have has come to me without seeking it out." So they retain their stubbornness and greed for material things, which makes them waste their lives.

I now have a more important concern than those raised in the past. Forgive me for overwhelming you with my doubts, but my complete trust in your wisdom makes me come to you for words and advice. For years I have been a captain, but now I think it is necessary to work as a sailor, and I am thinking about how to do it. I am reluctant to give up active life altogether. In fact, I would say that I do not want to at all; some of my capacities decrease as the days pass, but others increase. Do you think that there are no activities in which we older people can collaborate with our intellect when our bodies are already weak?

***

Seneca

I hope I can alleviate your concerns.

Some who have governed were of short stature, some without limbs, some blind, some with light-coloured eyes, some fat, in some cases very young, and some have been called out of retirement by urgency, but all governed with the strength of their mind, not by the strength of their arm. Therefore, there is no reason to abandon public activity because of age. It is like saying that the helmsman does not help to steer the ship because, while others climb the mast to lower the sails, others strain to tighten the ropes and others hurriedly empty the bilge water, he remains sitting at the helm. He does not do the same as the young people, but his work is better and more important.

The great problems of life are not resolved with physical strength, or activity and agility of the body, but with reflection, character and prudence. These virtues are not exclusive to the elderly, but are more frequently encountered with advancing years. You, for example, who have worked since your childhood, should not be pushed aside because at your age you cannot carry heavy weights with your arms or because you are no longer inclined to travel without rest. Let them listen to your words about what to do and how to do it.

In Sparta, those who occupied the highest magistracies would be your elders, those we would call old today.

If curiosity calls you to find out about the history of other countries, you will see that powerful States and large companies have been brought to catastrophe by the young, having been rescued by the old. Haste is the mark of youth, and prudence the mark of age.

They say that memory fades with age. There is no doubt about it, unless you exercise it frequently, or unless nature has blessed you with an unfading mind. For my part, I know not only the present generation, but also their parents and grandparents. I am not afraid of losing my memory by reading tombstones, contrary to superstition. Quite the opposite; by reading them I refresh my memory with the names of those who have left us. In fact, I don't know any elderly man who has forgotten where he keeps his money. They remember everything that is of interest to them: business meetings, who owes them money, and to whom they owe money. Think about lawyers, judges, doctors, professors, philosophers or writers when they are elderly. What a wealth of knowledge they treasure! Older people retain their intellect just by keeping their minds active and engaged in some work. And this is not only the case for great professions or important duties. It also applies to private life and quiet activities.

Sophocles composed tragedies well into old age, and his sons, fearing that he would lose his fortune because of his devotion to art, brought him before a judge to take away the administration of his property, accusing him of dementia, as would happen today if a doctor certified the illness. At the trial, Sophocles read to the court from the play he had finished in those days, Oedipus at Colonus, and asked them if they thought the play was written by someone with dementia. The verdict was that he was innocent.

Therefore, do not be afraid to continue cooperating while you still have your strength.

Printed in Great Britain
by Amazon